GOOD NEWS STUDIES

Consulting Editor: Robert J. Karris, O.F.M.

Volume 6

St. Paul's Corinth

Texts and Archaeology

by

Jerome Murphy-O'Connor

Introduction by

John H. Elliott

A Michael Glazier Book
THE LITURGICAL PRESS
Collegeville, Minnesota

A Michael Glazier Book
published by
THE LITURGICAL PRESS

Cover design by David Manahan, O.S.B.

4	5	6	7	8	9

Library of Congress Cataloging-in-Publication Data

Murphy-O'Connor, J. (Jerome), 1935-
    St. Paul's Corinth : text and archaeology / by Jerome Murphy
-O'Connor ; introduction by John H. Elliot.
        p.   cm.
    Reprint. Originally published: Wilmington, Del. : M. Glazier, 1983. (Good news studies ; v. 6).
    "A Michael Glazier book."
    Includes bibliographical references and indexes.
    ISBN 0-8146-5303-0
    1. Paul, the Apostle, Saint,—Journeys—Greece—Corinth.
2. Bible. N.T. Acts XVIII, 1-18—Antiquities. 3. Bible. N.T. Corinthians—Antiquities. 4. Corinth (Greece)—Antiquities.
5. Corinth (Greece)—Antiquities, Roman. 6. Corinth (Greece)-
-Description. 7. Greece—Antiquities. 8. Greece—Antiquities, Roman. 9. Excavations (Archaeology)—Greece—Corinth. I. Title.
II. Title: Saint Paul's Corinth. III. Series: Good news studies ; v. 6.
BS2506.M85   1990
227'.2095—dc20
                              90-38451
                                  CIP

For
Seán and Brigid Ronan
in gratitude

The Man from Delos

This bronze head of a man, dated about 80 B.C., was found in the gymnasium on Delos, and is now on exhibit at the National Museum, Athens. The identity of the sitter is unknown, but he was certainly a troubled individual. The plaintive, uncertain mouth, and the unhappy eyes reveal a personality beset by doubts and anxieties. The slightly upward glance looks into a void, as if all the familiar certainties had suddenly been perceived as illusions. The modelling of the furrowed brow and slack cheeks conveys a deep sense of loss and emptiness. He faces the future without faith or hope. It was men such as this who heeded Paul.

TABLE OF CONTENTS

PART 2: WHEN WAS PAUL IN CORINTH?

PART 3: ARCHAEOLOGY

INDICES

ILLUSTRATIONS

INTRODUCTION

This book is a tin mine! "Gold mine," of course, is the modern idiom but, as the reader shall soon learn, "tin mine" is a more appropriate image for data regarding a city renown for its bronzeware and "noisy gongs" (1 Corinthians 13:1).

Here is rich ore for a host of modern miners — a dazzling lode of literary and archeological information about one of the most celebrated cities of the ancient Mediterranean world and one of the most fascinating centers of the early Christian movement.

This volume is also a publishing first. At long last we have a book containing all that vital information on Corinth, its history, society and culture, which is generally unavailable to the layperson or buried in unfamiliar ancient texts, archaeological reports, or obscure exegetical footnotes. As the Bibliography shows, there are many informative, secondary studies of ancient Corinth. But until this text there has been no comprehensive collection of the primary source material available to the general reader in English translation. Now, however, we have evidence from twenty-one Greek and Latin authors arranged chronologically from the first century BC to the second century AD, the latest in pertinent archaeological data, and the fullest text to date of the Edict of Claudius together with a discussion of its bearing on the chronology of Paul and early Christianity. Here it is, gentle reader, now in one handy package: "Everything you always wanted to know about Corinth but didn't know where to find."

The relevance and significance of the material, however, cuts across academic disciplines and areas of interest. As we have come to expect of Fr. Murphy-O'Connor, he has once again provided us with diverse data for understanding "the big picture" — in this case Corinth in its historical, social and cultural totality. The data collected provide us with not only a physical but also a social and cultural map of Corinth, a map indispensable for charting the undulating course of the city's history, its role in the Mediterranean world, and its significance in the early Christian movement. So harken, all ye classicists, historians, scriptural exegetes, Bible readers, and tourists to Corinth! This vademecum will be as handy as your American Express card; don't leave home or your library without it.

With Murphy-O'Connor we are in the hands of a veteran guide. Author of numerous studies on Paul's Corinthian correspondence, international expert on the history, community and literature of Qumran, United Nations guide to the archaeological sites in Israel, Fr. Murphy-O'Connor brings to this work the experience and expertise of one who comprehends the interrelation of theology and culture, material reality and spiritual vision, proclamation and praxis in both ancient and modern contexts. Although assembly of the pertinent ancient evidence is his main concern, Murphy-O'Connor also shows in several instances how this data illuminates Paul's communication with the Corinthians and at points challenges dubious assumptions of the interpreters (e.g. sacred prostitution at Aphrodite's temple as the supposed backdrop for the sexual issues treated in 1 Corinthians 5-7). On the basis of a fresh examination of the Gallio inscription he is also able to show that Paul arrived in Corinth in the year 49 AD and was brought before Gallio, the Roman proconsul of Achaia, between July and October of the year 51 AD. Consequently greater certainty is gained concerning a key date in the Pauline chronology and, in turn, the chronology of the entire early Christian movement.

At the same time the data collected here provide us with a broader basis for a systemic perspective on the "larger Corinthian picture." Here we have a wealth of detail on the physical site of Corinth, its size, layout and environs; its social history, economy, commercial and military importance; the social scene itself, its mixed population, chief institutions, social structures and stratification; and the relation of all this to the social drama at Corinth at the time of Paul, the monuments of beliefs, values, and cultural traditions, the conflict of cultures, and the clash of Christian and non-Christian ideologies. Christian life at Corinth, according to Paul's letters, was marked by tensions and skirmishes within and without the community. The data collected here help sketch out the map of the physical and cultural terrain over which these battles were waged. While any analysis of the conflict must remain incomplete, at least we can better appreciate some of the positions taken by opposing forces when we are clearer about the landscape over which they fought.

With material like this at our disposal, we are thus better equipped to engage in the tasks of social description, sociological analysis, and sociological-theological integration of texts within their specific contexts. In the exegetical field, recent attempts at social description (e.g. Ronald F. Hock, *The Social Context of Paul's Ministry* [Philadelphia: Fortress, 1980]; Wayne A. Meeks, *The First Urban Christians* [New Haven: Yale University Press, 1982]) or cross-disciplinary analysis (e.g. Gerd Theissen, *The Social Setting of Pauline Christianity: Essays on Corinth* [Philadelphia: Fortress, 1982]; Bruce Malina, *The New Testament World. Insights from Cultural Anthropology* [Atlanta: John Knox Press, 1981]) are forging the way toward a more systemic conception of social scenes and a more integrated sociological-theological interpretation of scriptural texts-in-contexts. This collection of material and the further correlations made by its author serve the advance of such an approach while at the same time providing an extensive data base for evaluating its provisional conclusions, particularly in regard to Christian life at Corinth. In brief, this volume offers abundant evidence for advancing our reconstruction of Corinthian life and history and thereby recapturing that living context or "Sitz im Leben" within which, in particular, Christianity at this Roman colony "lived, and moved, and had its being."

Historical reconstruction, systemic sociological analysis, and sociological exegesis may all sound like enterprises reserved to the "experts." So one final comment on the utility of this book belongs to that proverbial person of pew, Joe or Mary average Bible reader. In trying to understand the ancient world and decipher its texts, particularly its religious literature, expert and layperson alike face the constant twin dangers of anachronism and ethnocentrism. In our concern for existential relevance and spiritual edification, we often inadvertently read into foreign literature meanings which derive rather from our modern world and our personal experience. In theological terms we are often guilty of confusing eisegesis with exegesis. Into texts "then and there" we import meanings derived from our "here and now." Unclear about specific geographical, social or cultural dimensions of an ancient city like Corinth, we compare this "Couch of Greece" and its life with that of any modern seaport or "Sin City, Everywhere." Then with such familiar modern categories as "religious versus secular," "spiritual versus material," or "ideal versus material reality" we attempt to decode Corinthian texts and discover absolute and enduring spiritual messages. In the process, however, we attain not clarity but confusion. For we have failed to appreciate the historical relativity and cultural specificity of the material we are attempting to understand.

The value of a book such as this one is that on the one hand it familiarizes us with a time and a place and a culture so alien from our own. With the detail presented here we can more clearly perceive the "lived, everyday reality" of Saint Paul's Corinth: the market place and the temples where the problem of food dedicated to idols arose (1 Cor. 8-10); the names of and reverence paid to those Corinthian deities —Apollo, Athena, Aphrodite, Aesclepius, Dionysus, Demeter and Core — idols, according to Paul, which had no real existence (1 Cor. 8:4-6); the famous Isthmian games and the local immediacy they lent to Paul's athletic metaphors of "running a race" and "not boxing as one beating the air" (1 Cor. 9:24-27); Corinth's mining, metallurgy and famed bronzeware which included bronze vases used in the theater as sounding instruments ("noisy gongs," 1 Cor. 13:1); the size and location of houses, illustrating the "house churches" where early Christians met and worshipped (1 Cor. 16:15-16; cf. ch 14); the mix of cultures and diversity of languages, and the inevitable problems of understanding words spoken in "foreign tongues" (1 Cor. 12-14). All such evidence and more makes the world of Corinthian Christianity come alive and confront the modern reader as an actual, lived episode of the human drama.

At the same time the material in this book illustrates the great distance between Paul's world and ours and thereby allows us to understand the Corinthians and Paul on their own historical, cultural, and religious terms. Thus the evidence collected here more fully situates early Christianity at Corinth in time and place, it more graphically concretizes life and social interaction there, and it gives a more physical human face to the spiritual message of the Christian literature associated with Saint Paul's Corinth.

With this volume the author has put many of us in his debt. With several other early Christian sites to explore, let us hope this kind of a study finds many successors.

John H. Elliott

FOREWORD

The Christian community at Corinth was but another touch of color in the variegated mosaic of a great city. Its members were not a foreign import; they came from the city and were conditioned by its tone and temper, by its history and institutions. The more we know of Corinth, therefore, the better we are likely to understand the people whose theological searching inspired two of the most important of Paul's letters. It is unlikely, for example, that the different groups mentioned by Paul (1 Cor 1:12) developed out of purely logical discussions. Social, economic, and educational factors contributed to the formation of individuals predisposed to view reality in a particular way.

A complete analysis of these factors would involve writing the social history of Corinth in the 1st cent. A.D. At this stage such a project would be premature both on methodological and factual grounds. Discussion has been inaugurated on the proper methodology (Carney, 1975, 1979), but it will be some time before a consensus emerges. In terms of the factual base, important work has been done on the history (Wiseman, 1979), inscriptions (Kent), religions (Lisle; Smith, 1977), and numismatics (Bagdikian), but despite Larsen's contribution on economics and trade, much still needs to be done in this area as in others. Moreover, what has been accomplished needs to be completed and brought up to date by new discoveries.

In Part 1 I have sought to aid in this task by bringing together all the major references to Corinth in the works of Greek and Latin authors from the 1st cent. B.C. to the 2nd cent. A.D. Some of the information they supply has already been exploited, but many of the aspects they reveal have been passed over in silence, and the hints they throw out have not been followed up. The accompanying commentaries are not intended to be exhaustive; they are designed only to clarify the meaning or to highlight the importance or implications of what is being said. If at times the sociological relevance has been underlined, there has been no systematic attempt to develop the sociological inferences. Such sociological exegesis (Elliott: 10) can be undertaken profitably only when the data base is complete. What has been done, however, is to confront the literary evidence with the results of the excavations of Corinth, Isthmia, and Cenchreae. Thus ruins are enlivened by the words of eye-witnesses, and their descriptions are given a concrete dimension.

Part 2 deals with the documentary evidence for the dates of the Edict of Claudius and the term of office of Gallio as proconsul of Achaia. I have no new hypotheses to propose, but feel that the texts should be included in any collection of material relevant to Corinth, particularly since the full text of the Gallio inscription from Delphi is not as well known as it should be.

Part 3 is more directly archaeological, and is designed to highlight the importance of non-literary data. By far the greatest amount of new material falls into this category, and there is the very real danger that, as time goes on, existing hypotheses will account for less and less of the evidence unless such data is incorporated (Meyers and Strange: 19-30). This observation has particular force as regards Corinth, because little, if any, of the vast body of information accumulated by the generations of dedicated American scholars who have dug at Corinth has found its way into New Testament introductions and commentaries. Without being in any way exhaustive, I have tried to redress the balance by drawing attention to a number of physical factors which are important for a correct understanding of Paul's ministry there.

On a much more personal level this book attempts to share the pleasure I experienced in discovering a world about which I knew very little. My curiosity was excited and my imagination stimulated in a way that I had never anticipated. My only hope is that it will do something of the same for others. My pleasure was enhanced by the willingness with which friends responded to requests for aid. My brother, Brian Murphy-O'Connor, and Caroline Florimont produced the drawings adapted from the excavation reports of the American School of Classical Studies at Athens. George MacRae, S.J. obtained permission for me to use the translations from the Loeb Classical Library whose copyright is held by the President and Fellows of Harvard University. Bentley Layton procured the translation of the passage from Aelius Aristides. John H. Elliott read parts of the first draft and, as usual, made a number of extremely helpful comments. To all I express my deepest gratitude. My greatest debt, however, is to H. E. Seán Ronan, Irish Ambassador to Greece and Israel, and to his wife, Brigid. I first visited Greece at their invitation, and it was their generous hospitality on two occasions which made it possible for me to visit Corinth and to work in the library of the American School of Classical Studies at Athens. The dedication of this book to them is but very inadequate repayment.

Jerome Murphy-O'Connor, O.P.
Ecole Biblique de Jérusalem
November, 1982.

For the opportunity to add new material to this second edition, I am deeply grateful to my new publisher, The Liturgical Press. The most important supplement comes from the *Metamorphoses* or *Golden Ass* of Apuleius, a novel which offers perhaps the most realistic picture of lower-class daily life in the Greece of Paul's day. But there are also additions from Juvenal, Livy, Martial, Philostratus, and the *Greek Anthology.*

Ecole Biblique de Jérusalem
October, 1990.

PART 1
THE ANCIENT TEXTS

Introduction

Most New Testament introductions and commentaries on Paul's letters to the Corinthians contain an account of the city's history. One of the great commercial centers of the eastern Mediterranean, it was destroyed by the Romans in 146 B.C. and refounded as a colony by Julius Caesar in 44 B.C. Thus, there were in fact two Corinths, one Greek and the other Roman, each with its distinctive institutions and ethos.

Our knowledge of the details of this history derives from scattered allusions in a score of Greek and Latin authors ranging from the 1st cent. B.C. to the 2nd cent. A.D. The references can be found in any number of scientific works, but the texts themselves are rarely quoted, and the works from which they are drawn are not always easily available. In consequence, serious students are forced to rely on second-hand information; they have to be content with a summary. Now, no matter how cleverly a summary is done it can never be a substitute for the original sources. Their immediacy, vigor, and charm are necessarily sacrificed to a concentration on the essentials. A summary can offer the most important hard facts, but it cannot communicate the life of a city. For that we have to look at first-hand accounts which reflect, not only the mood inspired in the writer, but the small' things which caught their fancy and which remained graven on their memories of Corinth.

In order to appreciate this dimension, however, a text has to be read right through. This is why I have chosen to present the passages in terms of their authors rather than in terms of a topical or chronological framework. The unfortunate consequence is a certain amount of repetitiousness. Moreover, the data on a given point appears in a number of different places. These disadvantages, however, are easily transformed into benefits. The personal assemblage of data permits a critical assessment, and repetitiousness raises the important questions of sources and traditional themes.

The authors are presented in chronological order with the exception of Pausanias. He visited Corinth a century after Paul, but his text is the earliest guide-book to the city and the surrounding area. Thus, when read in conjunction with the maps and plans, it sets the scene in the most authentic way possible. His account is so detailed that it enables us to visualize the roads and places that most of his predecessors did not bother to describe.

The framework of the section devoted to each author is substantially the same. It opens with a brief presentation of the writer's life in which particular attention is paid to the nature of the work from which the citation is taken, and to the question of whether he actually visited Corinth. The text is then quoted at length, and is followed by a commentary. The function of the latter is to heighten the intelligibility of the text, and also, when necessary, to raise critical questions concerning the reliability or completeness of the information.

In the case of long accounts, notably those of Strabo and Pausanias, I have been obliged to break the text up into sense-units introduced by their own sub-headings and followed by a commentary. Otherwise, the commentary would have been too far away to be really useful. I have also found it more appropriate to integrate a very brief quotation from one author into the commentary on another when the context makes it more meaningful than a separate comment.

PAUSANIAS

All that is known about Pausanias is the little that can be inferred from occasional remarks in his *Description of Greece*. He was apparently a native of western Asia Minor, and may have turned to medicine after being forced to abandon his study of Homer. The fifth volume of his book was being written in A.D. 174 (cf. p. 41 below), and the work was finished or the author had died before A.D. 180 (Jones: ix-x). It is thought that he visited Corinth not long after A.D. 165 (Wiseman, 1979:508; cf. Comfort: 314).

The *Description of Greece* is a guide-book, the first of its kind. It was designed, not for the armchair traveller, but for those who took the trouble to visit the places mentioned. It directs visitors to the things worth seeing, but does not describe what they could see for themselves. The frequent references to 'guides' (*exegetai*) implies that there were locals who, for a consideration, could supply more detailed information. Pausanias used sources and consulted experts, but there is no doubt that he travelled all the roads he describes.

The section on Corinth is found in Book 2 of Pausanias' ten-volume work. The standard reference system, found in the Loeb translation, divides each book into chapters and paragraphs; thus, 1.3 means paragraph three of chapter one. I have added sub-titles in order to underline the methodical way in which Pausanias organises his information. He moves from the region to the center of the city, and then explores the chief roads radiating out from this point.

In the century which intervened between Paul's visit and that of Pausanias, Corinth had been hit by a massive earthquake in A.D. 77 (Wiseman, 1979:506) which necessitated rebuilding much of the city. In addition, many new buildings and monuments were added during the 2nd cent. A.D. Thus, the city described by Pausanias was in many ways different from the one that Paul knew. However, the dedication of the generations of scholars who have excavated in the Corinthia since 1896 under the auspices of the American

School of Classical Studies at Athens has now made it possible to determine which of the buildings and monuments mentioned by Pausanias were in existence in the middle of the 1st cent. A.D. Such archaeological data will be integrated at appropriate points in the commentary.

The strangest aspect of Pausanias' account, as far as the modern reader is concerned, is the attention he accords to local cults, myths, and legends. The immediate temptation is to skip this material and jump to the factual data, for the arbitrary character of mythological association needs no emphasis. However, the historical roots of a myth are of much less importance than the fact that Pausanias opens for us the thought-world of the ancient Corinthians. Not all Paul's contemporaries would have been as erudite as our author, but many of the myths he mentions would have come to mind unconsciously as they travelled through the region. The legends would have both revealed the darker side of their nature and focused their highest aspirations.

DESCRIPTION OF GREECE, 2:1.1-5.5

Introduction

1.1 The Corinthian land is a portion of the Argive, and is named after Corinthus. That Corinthus was a son of Zeus I have never known anybody say seriously except the majority of the Corinthians. Eumelus, the son of Amphilytus, of the family of the Bacchiadae, who is said to have composed the epic poem, says in his Corinthian History (if indeed the history be his) that Ephyra, the daughter of Oceanus, dwelt first in this land; that afterwards Marathon, the son of Epopeus, the son of Aloeus, the son of Helius (*Sun*), fleeing from the lawless violence of his father migrated to the sea coast of Attica; that on the death of Epopeus he came to Peloponnesus, divided his kingdom among his sons, and returned to Attica; and that Asopia was renamed after Sicyon, and Ephyraea after Corinthus.

While to begin at the beginning is a good principle, it does seem a little exaggerated to start with the mythological origins of Corinth. The popular view, which underlines the opinion the Corinthians had of their city and guarantees that Pausanias listened to locals, is contrasted with the information provided by Eumelos, an epic poet of the 8th cent. B.C. who is said to have belonged to the Bacchiadae, the oligarchy which ruled Corinth in the 8-7th cents. B.C. He traces the origin of the city to Sun and Sea, both of which are still undeniable factors in the environment.

> 1.2 Corinth is no longer inhabited by any of the old Corinthians, but by colonists sent out by the Romans. This change is due to the Achaean League. The Corinthians, being members of it, joined in the war against the Romans, which Critolaus, when appointed general of the Achaeans, brought about by persuading to revolt both the Achaeans and the majority of the Greeks outside the Peloponnesus. When the Romans won the war, they carried out a general disarmament of the Greeks and dismantled the walls of such cities as were fortified. Corinth was laid waste by Mummius, who at that time commanded the Romans in the field, and it is said that it was afterwards refounded by Caesar, who was the author of the present constitution of Rome. Carthage, too, they say, was refounded in his reign.

Despite its eminent origins Corinth did not enjoy an uninterrupted history. After its destruction by the Romans in 146 B.C. it was refounded by Julius Caesar in 44 B.C. as a Roman colony. It had been derelict, though not entirely unoccupied (cf. p. 48), for just over a century. If inscriptions are any indication, Greek would have reestablished itself as the official language of the city by the time of Pausanias, but at the time of Paul it was still Latin; "of the 104 texts which are prior to the reign of Hadrian [A.D. 117-138] 101 are in Latin and only three in Greek, a virtual monopoly for the Latin language." (Kent: 19). Though it would be exagger-

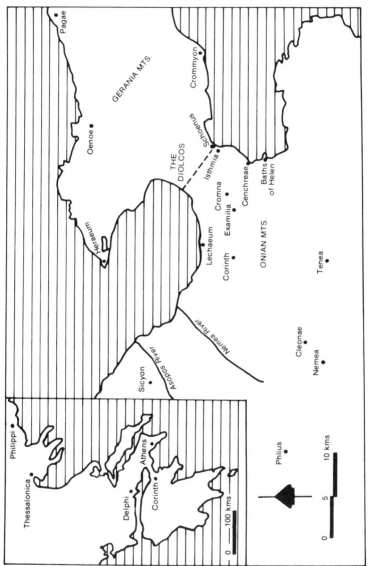

Fig. 1. The Corinthia.

ated to claim that there were no Greeks in the city that Paul knew or that their language was unknown to the inhabitants — he did after all write in Greek — the structure and administration of Corinth was Roman. Inscriptions show that its official title was *Colonia Laus Julia Corinthiensis* (Kent, 60, 70), and that from the beginning "the colony was organized on a tri-partite basis of an assembly of citizen voters, a city council, and annual magistrates; her civic government, which continued to function without any major changes until early Byzantine times, thus conformed to a pattern typical of the great majority of Roman *coloniae*, and was in effect a miniature replica of the government of Republican Rome." (Kent: 23).

Strabo gives more details of the failure of the Achaean League and the devastation of Corinth (cf. p. 66 below).

The Isthmus

1.3 In the Corinthian territory is also the place called Crommyon from Cromus the son of Poseidon. Here they say that Phaea was bred; overcoming this sow was one of the traditional achievements of Theseus. Farther on the pine still grew by the shore at the time of my visit, and there was an altar of Melicertes. At this place, they say, the boy was brought ashore by a dolphin; Sisyphus found him lying and gave him burial on the Isthmus, establishing the Isthmian games in his honour.

1.4 At the beginning of the Isthmus is the place where the brigand Sinis used to take hold of pine trees and draw them down. All those whom he overcame in fight he used to tie to the trees, and then allow them to swing up again. Thereupon each of the pines used to drag to itself the bound man, and as the bond gave way in neither direction but was stretched equally in both, he was torn in two. This was the way in which Sinis himself was slain by Theseus. For Theseus rid of evildoers the road from Troezen to Athens, killing those whom I have enumerated and, in sacred Epidaurus, Periphetes, thought to be the son of Hephaestus, who used to fight with a bronze club.

The full legend of Theseus is given by Plutarch (c. A.D. 46-120) in a work by that name. Determined to emulate Heracles this son of Aegeus or Poseidon travelled along the edge of the Saronic Gulf from Troezen in the extreme eastern part of the Peloponnese to Athens, engaging in a series of ferocious single-handed combats with dangerous men and beasts. His route was the reverse of that followed by Pausanias who comes first to Crommyon (cf. fig. 1), today the village of Hagios Theodoros.

Fleeing from her husband Athamas, the cruel stepmother Ino jumped into the sea carrying her son Melicertes. They were transformed into the deities Leucothea, the foam-goddess, and Palaemon ('the Wrestler'). Other monuments to the former (1.9), to the latter (1.8), and to both (2.1; 3.4) are mentioned subsequently.

The legendary Sisyphus was styled by Homer as "the most crafty of men" (*Iliad,* 6:154), and became the type of the cunning trickster. He foiled a cattle rustler by attaching lead plates stamped 'stolen by Autolycus' to the hooves of his beasts, enabling him to follow them easily. He played his most famous trick on Death. Having previously arranged with his wife to give him no funeral dues, he prevailed on Death to permit him to return to earth from Hades in order to remonstrate. Whereupon he neglected to return until he died of old age. According to one version, this is why Death decided to keep him busy so that he could not run away again. Sisyphus was condemned to push a rock to the top of a hill, but each time just as he neared the summit it slipped from his hands and he had to start all over again. Another, less complimentary, reason for this punishment is given below by Pausanias at 5.1.

According to Pausanias, Sisyphus had been king of Corinth (3.11), having received the kingdom from Medea. The reason for this gift is not explained, and one cannot but help feeling that our author was concerned to find some explanation (cf. 4.1) of the importance that Sisyphus had for Corinth. Not only did he have a temple by the spring on Acrocorinth (5:1; cf. Strabo, p. 60 below), but he was buried on the Isthmus (2.2), where he had received the body of Melicertes/Palaemon. For those of Paul's contemporaries who felt the absurdity of human existence as keenly as the Man from Delos (cf. frontispiece) Sisyphus would have been a very powerful symbol. The futility of his task in Hades —success was never possible — would have focused the sense of emptiness of those whose interior world was filled with anxiety and uncertainty and who faced the future without faith or hope. The temporary success of the trickster was the most that could be envisioned. The Corinthians' awareness of this spiritual void to a great extent explains their receptivity to Paul's preaching.

> 1.5 The Corinthian Isthmus stretches on the one hand to the sea at Cenchreae, and on the other to the sea at Lechaeum. For this is what makes the region to the south mainland. He who tried to make the Peloponnesus an island gave up before digging through the Isthmus. Where they began to dig is still to be seen, but into the rock they did not advance at all. So it is still mainland as its nature is to be. Alexander the son of Philip wished to dig through Mimas, and his attempt to do this was his only unsuccessful project. The Cnidians began to dig through their isthmus, but the Pythian priestess stopped them. So difficult is it for man to alter by violence what Heaven has made.
>
> 1.6 A legend of the Corinthians about their land is not peculiar to them, for I believe that the Athenians were the first to relate a similar story to glorify Attica. The Corinthians say that Poseidon had a dispute with Helius (*Sun*) about the land, and that Briareos arbitrated between them, assigning to Poseidon the Isthmus and the parts adjoining, and giving to Helius the height above the city.

For the location of Cenchreae and Lechaeum see fig. 1. The exact width of the Isthmus at its narrowest point is 5950 meters (Frazer: 6), and very early the Corinthians had perceived the enormous advantages of a canal joining the

Corinthian and Saronic Gulfs. The reasons are eloquently presented by Strabo (p. 54 below). Pausanias' allusion is to Nero, the only one to actually begin excavations; more details are given by Suetonius, *Nero,* 19.2 (p. 114 below). What Pausanias saw is an accurate description of the eastern end of Nero's canal; a cutting was made through the alluvial soil but stopped at the conglomerate schist (Frazer: 7-8). We can be sure, therefore, that his route from Crommyon to Isthmia followed the shore of the Saronic Gulf.

Pausanias was apparently unaware of previous projects to cut a canal through the Isthmus; see Pliny the Elder, *Natural History,* 4:9-11 (p. 86 below). His two parallels come from Asia Minor. In the 6th cent. B.C. the Cnidians tried to preserve themselves from the Persians by cutting off their peninsula from the mainland; it is located just north of Rhodes and contains the modern Turkish town of Knidos. Alexander the Great's project in the 4th cent. B.C. concerned the peninsula running north-south between Izmir and the island of Chios. Mimas is the present Bos Dagh.

A hint of the long-standing rivalry between Athens and Corinth (cf. p. 58 below) appears in the two versions of the dispute between Poseidon and the Sun. The adjudicator, Briareos, was one of the three sons of Heaven and Earth known as the Hecatoncheires, the hundred-handed monsters. The height is, of course, Acrocorinth which the Sun awarded to Aphrodite (cf. 4.6).

The Sanctuary of Poseidon at Isthmia

1.7 Ever since, they say, the Isthmus has belonged to Poseidon. Worth seeing here are a theatre and a white-marble stadium. Within the sanctuary of the god stand on the one side portrait statues of athletes who have won victories at the Isthmian games, on the other side pine trees growing in a row, the greater number of them rising up straight. On the temple, which is not very large, stand bronze Tritons. In the fore-temple are images, two of Poseidon, a third of Amphitrite, and a Sea, which also is of bronze. The offerings inside were dedicated in our time by Herodes the Athenian, four horses, gilded except for the hoofs, which are of ivory, and two gold Tritons, beside the horses, with the parts below the waist of ivory. 1.8 On the car stand Amphitrite and Poseidon, and there is the boy Palaemon upright upon a dolphin. These too are made of ivory and gold. On the middle of the base on which the car is has been wrought a Sea holding up the young Aphrodite, and on either side are the nymphs called Nereids.

I know that there are altars to these in other parts of Greece, and that some Greeks have even dedicated to them precincts by shores, where honours are also paid to Achilles. In Gabala is a holy sanctuary of Doto, where there was still remaining the robe with which the Greeks say that Eriphyle was bribed to wrong her son Alcmaeon. 1.9 Among the reliefs on the base of the statue of Poseidon are the sons of Tyndareus, because these too are saviours of ships and of sea-faring men. The other offerings are images of Calm and of Sea, a horse like a whale from the breast onward, Ino and Bellerophontes, and the horse Pegasus.

2.1 Within the enclosure is on the left a temple of Palaemon, with images in it of Poseidon, Leucothea, and Palaemon himself. There is also what is called his Holy of Holies, and an underground descent to it, where they say that Palaemon is concealed. Whosoever, whether Corinthian or stranger, swears falsely here, can by no means escape from his oath. There is also an ancient sanctuary called the altar of Cyclopes, and they sacrifice to the Cyclopes upon it.

2.2 The graves of Sisyphus and of Neleus — for they say that Neleus came to Corinth, died of disease, and was buried near the Isthmus — I do not think that anyone would look for after reading Eumelus. For he says that not even to Nestor did Sisyphus show the tomb of Neleus, because it must be kept unknown to everybody alike, and that Sisyphus is indeed buried on the Isthmus, but that few Corinthians, even those of his own day, knew where the grave was.

The shrine of Poseidon at Isthmia is located in fig. 1, and the arrangement of the sanctuary and its relation to the theatre and the stadium are depicted in fig. 2.

Unfortunately, Pausanias is here more concerned with statues than with buildings because it seems likely that most of the objects he mentions were not in existence at the time of Paul. One is explicitly credited to Herodes the Athenian (A.D. 101-177), who has been characterized as "the last great patron of ancient art to have good taste" (Levi: 131), and excavations have revealed that the disposition of the sanctuary underwent considerable modifications in the first part of the 2nd cent. A.D.

In the 1st cent. A.D. the temple was surrounded by a simple wall. On three sides the width of the space between the two was only 8 meters, hardly enough for the lines of pines and portrait statues mentioned by Pausanias. The main entrance to the enclosure was on the east, and just inside to the south stood a square altar (Broneer, 1973:68-75). At this period the only structure that can be connected with the cult of Palaemon was a sacrificial pit in the center of a square delimited by a wall; it lay outside the south wall of the sanctuary of Poseidon (Broneer, 1973:100).

The stadium was remodelled in the early 1st cent. A.D. and therefore apparently underwent no further changes (Broneer, 1973:66). The theatre was most likely in ruins at the time of Paul, because the first Roman reconstruction is dated to A.D. 66 or 67, presumably in anticipation of the visit of Nero who fancied himself on his singing (Gebhard, 141); cf. p. 115 below. No hippodrome is mentioned by Pausanias, but that he knew of one is indicated by a remark elsewhere, "Glaukos son of Sisyphus at the Isthmus is also a Horse-scarer" (6:20.19). Apparently in most hippodromes there was a place where the horses inexplicably took fright and caused accidents; at this point the charioteers were careful "to offer sacrifices and to pray to the Horse-scarer to be kind to them" (6:20.15). The hippodrome at Isthmia is hypothetically located 2 kms south-west of the temple of Poseidon (Broneer, 1973:121), but no date has been suggested.

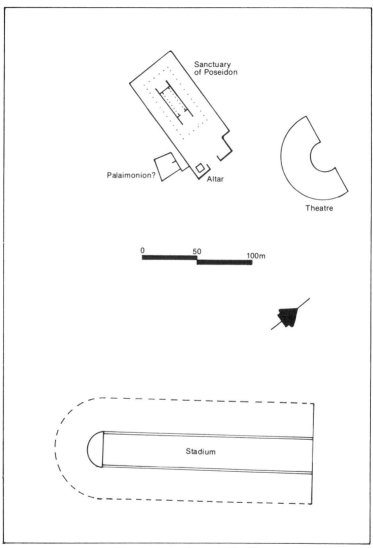

Fig. 2. Isthmia c. A.D. 50

The Isthmian Games

> 2.2 The Isthmian Games were not interrupted even when
> Corinth had been laid waste by Mummius, but so long as
> it lay deserted the celebration of the games was entrusted
> to the Sicyonians, and when it was rebuilt the honour was
> restored to the present inhabitants.

The Isthmian games were one of the four great panhellenic festivals; it ranked below the Olympic Games but above those celebrated at Delphi and Nemea. Initiated in the early 6th cent. B.C. the Isthmian games took place every two years in the spring. After the sack of Corinth in 146 B.C. control of the games passed to the neighboring town of Sicyon, 10 kms north-west of Corinth. Pausanias does not say that the games themselves were transferred to the stadium at Sicyon, but such was in fact the case. The games were not celebrated at Isthmia when Strabo visited the Corinthia in 29 B.C. (cf. p. 55 below), and excavations have shown that the temple of Poseidon lay abandoned and in ruins in the immediate pre-Roman period (Broneer, 1973:4).

As a matter of principle the new Roman colony established in 44 B.C. must have claimed the games from the beginning. The economic advantages to be drawn from the enormous crowds who attended were not to be despised. However, to host the games demanded a considerable financial outlay, and none of the new settlers was in a position to assume that burden. Within fifty years the situation had changed; many Corinthians had become extremely wealthy, for the very reasons laid out by Strabo (cf. p. 55 below). An inscription reveals not only the name of the individual who brought the games back to Isthmia but also what it must have cost him. "[To Lucius Castricius Regulus, son of _____, of the tribe _____, aedile, prefect *iure dicundo*], duovir, quinquennial duovir, agonothete of the Isthmian and the Caesarean games, who was [the first] to preside over the Isthmian games at the Isthmus under the sponsorship of Colonia Laus Julia Corinthiensis. He introduced [poetry contests in honor of] the divine Julia Augusta, and [a contest for] girls, and after all the buildings of the Caesarea were renovated, he [quickly(?)] completed [the construction of a stoa(?)], and gave a banquet for all the inhabitants of the colony. His son [Lucius] Castricius Regulus (erected this monument) to his father in accordance with a decree of the city council." (Kent: 70).

Corinth recovered administration of the Isthmian games sometime between 7 B.C. and A.D. 3 (Kent, 28), and the above inscription underlines how much rebuilding was necessary. The president of the games would have had to defray these costs from his personal fortune — and he was still able to offer free food and drink to all citizens! See Plutarch, p. 101f. below.

It will be noted that the above inscription mentions the Caesarean games in addition to the Isthmian games. Introduced in 30 B.C., these were held every fourth year in honour of the reigning Roman emperor. Thus, they coincided with every second celebration of the Isthmian games. Under Tiberius (A.D. 14-37) a further series of contests was added to the combined games. Such innovations highlight the strength of the Roman presence in Greece, but the resentment engendered by interference with a major festival with long-standing traditions must have intensified Greek national consciousness, which was one of the by-products of the panhellenic games. What Isokrates said at Olympia in the early 4th cent. B.C. remained true, "Now the founders of our great festivals are justly praised for handing down to us a custom by which, having proclaimed a truce and resolved our quarrels, we come together in one place, where, as we make our prayers and sacrifices in common, we are reminded of the kinship which exists among us and are made to feel more kindly towards each other for the future, reviving our old friendships and establishing new ties." (cf. Aelius Aristides, p. 122 below) Who can say what this spirit contributed to Paul's idea of Christian unity? In addition, it would be unrealistic to imagine that the contacts made during the Isthmian games contributed nothing to the spread of Christianity in Greece.

A good illustration of the extent of participation in the panhellenic games, as well as striking confirmation of the introduction of events for women by L. Castricius Regulus in the Isthmian games, is provided by an inscription from Delphi. "Hermesianax, son of Dionysios, of Caesarea Tralles, [Athens and Delphi], (dedicated) to Pythian Apollo his own daughters having the same citizenship: *Tryphosa* successively winner of the 200 meters at the Pythian games under the presidencies of Antigonos and Cleomachida, and at the Isthmian games under the presidency of Iuventius Proclus. First of the Virgins; *Hedea* winner of the race for war-chariots at the Isthmian games under the presidency of Cornelius Pulcher, and of the 200 meters both at the Nemean games under the presidency of Antigonos and at the Sicyonian games under the presidency of Menoeta; she carried away the prize for young lyre-players at the Sebastea in Athens under the presidency of Novus son of Philinius,...; *Dionysia* winner of the 200 meters at the Isthmian games under the presidency of Antigonos and at the Asklepian games in sacred Epidaurus under the presidency of Nicoteles." (G. Dittenberger, *Sylloge Inscriptionum Graecarum*, 3rd. ed., n. 802).

From the 3rd cent. B.C. on an increasing number of athletes competed primarily for financial rewards, and it seems likely that these young ladies were quasi-professionals whose abilities guaranteed their family a very good living. The presence of professionals, however, did not deter amateurs who were often victorious. There is nothing surprising in female participation in the 200 meters, but the fact that women raced war-chariots at Isthmia — Hedea would have won her race in A.D. 43 (Kent: 29) — certainly goes a long way towards explaining the liberated Corinthian women that Paul encountered (cf. 1 Cor 11:2-16).

Paul could not have been unaware of the Isthmian games, and was probably in Corinth when they took place; they were celebrated in the spring of A.D. 49 and 51. Athletic metaphors were a commonplace in the popular philosophy of the period (Pfitzner: 23-37), but it can hardly be coincidence that Paul's first sustained development of this theme occurs in a letter to the Corinthians (1 Cor 9:24-27). This conclusion is strengthened by the contrast he draws between 'the incorruptible crown,' which is the reward of Christian virtue, and 'the corruptible crown' given to victors in the games, because we have evidence to show that "the celery of the crown given to the victors in the Isthmian Games was withered, in contrast to the Nemean crown made from fresh celery plants" (Broneer, 1971:186; cf. p. 103 below). It is difficult to decide if Paul himself attended the games. Palestinian Jewish opposition to such spectacles is well documented (Schürer: 54-55), but we cannot assume that the same attitude prevailed in the Diaspora. If Philo felt himself free to attend an all-in wrestling contest (*Quod omnis probus,* 26) we can be sure that many Hellenized Jews had no compunction about attending the games. Jews had specially reserved seats in the theatre at Miletus in western Asia Minor (Smallwood, 1981; 510). Finally, it must be kept in mind that the vast numbers of non-Corinthians who came for the games were accommodated in tents, and that Paul's trade was that of a tentmaker (Acts 18:3 — cf. p. 176 below).

The Harbours of Corinth

2.3 The names of the Corinthian harbours were given them by Leches and Cenchrias, said to be the children of Poseidon and Peirene the daughter of Acheloüs, though in the poem called *The Great Eoeae* Peirene is said to be the daughter of Oebalus.

In Lechaeum are a sanctuary and a bronze image of Poseidon, and on the road leading from the Isthmus to Cenchreae a temple and ancient wooden image of Artemis. In Cenchreae are a temple and a stone statue of Aphrodite, after it on the mole running into the sea a bronze image of Poseidon, and at the other end of the harbour sanctuaries of Asclepius and of Isis. Right opposite Cenchreae is Helen's Bath. It is a large stream of salt, tepid water, flowing from a rock into the sea.

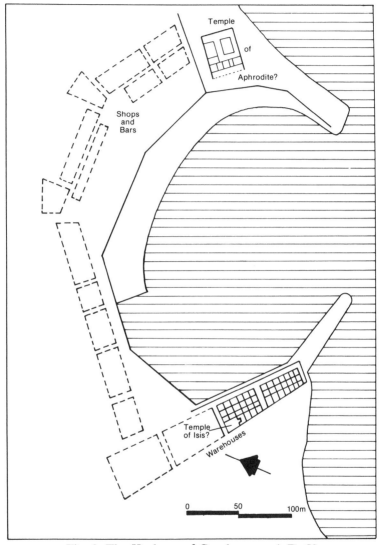

Temple of Aphrodite?

Shops and Bars

Temple of Isis?

Warehouses

0   50   100m

Fig. 3. The Harbour of Cenchreae c. A.D. 50.

For the location of Lechaeum, Cenchreae, and Helen's Bath see fig. 1.

Little is known about Lechaeum, because it has never been excavated. The validity of Pausanias' information for the 1st cent. A.D. is open to question because Plutarch may have seen something different (*Moralia,* 146D — cf. p. 105 below).

Paul knew Cenchreae well. Not only did he sail from there (Acts 18:18), but the town had a Christian community directed by Phoebe (Rom 16:1), and it would be unrealistic to imagine that he was not a frequent visitor. Though now mostly underwater, the harbour of his day can be reconstructed with a high degree of accuracy (fig. 3). Work on the harbour must have begun shortly after the establishment of the colony in 44 B.C. In fact, the Romans had to rebuild the port facilities completely; the two moles were completed early in the 1st cent. A.D. (Scranton et al.: 22-23).

The note of what Pausanias saw along the road would seem to make it certain that he travelled directly from Isthmia to Cenchreae (4 kms). However, we do not know where he entered the town. There is really no reason to assume that he came along the coast. Yet it is on this assumption that the identification of the large building in the upper part of fig. 3 as the temple of Aphrodite is based (Scranton et al.: 87). The outline shown on the plan is that of an edifice erected in the last years of the 1st cent. B.C. (Scranton et al.: 82) and destroyed by the earthquake of A.D. 77 (Scranton et al.: 87). It has a series of rooms around two sides of an open court; a disposition that is not incompatible with the private dwelling of a wealthy commercial magnate.

On the other side of the harbour at least four blocks of warehouses fronted the wharf against which the ships stern docked. Each block was divided longitudinally into a set of rooms opening on the front and another set on the rear; they were separated by one or two interior rooms whose purpose cannot be determined (Scranton et al.:41). In the early 1st cent. A.D. two rooms of one of the blocks were adapted to provide a small courtyard with a quadrangular niche in one

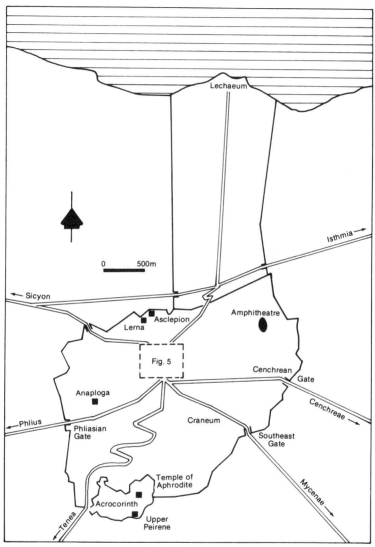

Fig. 4. The City of Corinth.

side. Some religious purpose seems the most natural hypothesis (Scranton et al.: 70-73). Whether at this period it was a sanctuary of Isis, as the excavators suggest, is open to doubt.

Ringing the harbour between the moles were a series of commercial buildings divided by streets. They seem to have been the sort of tabernae or shops that one finds in any small Greek port today (Scranton et al.: 36).

The dimensions of the harbour — 30,000 sq. meters (Scranton et al.: 14) — hardly justifies the description given by Apuleius (born c. A.D. 123), "the most famous town of all the Corinthians...a great and mighty haven with the ships of many a sundry nation" (*Metamorphoses*, 10:35), particularly when it is contrasted with Lechaeum whose inner harbour alone comprised 100,000 sq. meters (Scranton et al.: 14).

Helen's Bath, lying 1.6 kms south of Cenchreae, is still as Pausanias described it. The fact that he does not mention any building would appear to suggest that the massive ruin (Levi: 134) is of later construction.

The Road from Cenchreae to Corinth

2.4 As one goes up to Corinth are tombs, and by the gate is buried Diogenes of Sinope, whom the Greek surname the Dog. Before the city is a grove of cypresses called Craneum. Here are a precinct of Bellerophontes, a temple of Aphrodite Melaenis and the grave of Lais, upon which is set a lioness holding a ram in her fore-paws.

2.5 There is in Thessaly another tomb which claims to be that of Lais, for she went to that country also when she fell in love with Hippostratus. The story is that she was originally of Hycara in Sicily. Taken captive while yet a girl by Nicias and the Athenians, she was sold and brought to Corinth, where she surpassed in beauty the courtezans of her time, and so won the admiration of the Corinthians that even now they claim Lais as their own.

Only 9 kms separated Cenchreae from the agora of Corinth, but there were two ancient roads (Wiseman,

1978:64). A secondary road followed the north flank of Mt. Onium to the Southeast Gate of Corinth. The main road, presumably that followed by Paul and Pausanias, climbed gently through a fertile valley to Cromna where it joined the Isthmian Road coming from the sanctuary of Poseidon; it continued through Examilia and entered Corinth by the Cenchrean Gate (cf. fig. 1). Tombs have been noted along this road; many are of the Roman period but none have been accurately dated (Wiseman, 1978:68-69). While these caught Pausanias' eye, he fails to mention the quarries which line the road between Cromna and Examilia; these were opened in the 4th cent. B.C. but how long they continued in use is an open question (Wiseman, 1978:68).

It is curious that Pausanias first notes that the tomb of Diogenes is 'by the gate' and then locates Craneum as being 'before the city.' The impression is given that Craneum is further from the city than the tomb. But, were this the case, Craneum would have been encountered first. Hence, we must infer that the tomb was just *inside* the Cenchrean Gate, and that Craneum is to be sought in a relatively open area between the wall and the built-up section around the agora (cf. fig. 4). From Xenophon (c. 430-354 B.C.) we know that it was close enough to the agora for an uproar in the latter to be heard, and that it was in the vicinity of the lower slopes of Acrocorinth (*Hellenica*, 4:4.2-5). That Craneum was in an elevated area by reference to the rest of the city is confirmed by the remark of Theophrastus (372/369-288/285 B.C.) that it had 'crisp clean air' (*De causis plant.*, 5:14.2). We have to think, therefore, of a spacious park-like suburb, which was the most desirable residential and recreational area in Corinth, as one of Paul's contemporaries implies. Consoling an exile Plutarch wrote, "That you do not live in Sardis is nothing; neither do all Athenians live in Collytus, all Corinthians in Craneum, all Laconians in Pitane." (*Moralia*, 601B). It may be fanciful, but certainly not impossible, to imagine Paul going there to rest a while and look out over the city that had become his responsibility.

It is not certain that Diogenes (c. 400-325 B.C.) died in Corinth or even that he had lived there. It was widely believed, however, that it was at Craneum that he lived in a barrel and encountered Alexander the Great (*Diogenes Laertius*, 6:2.77; Plutarch, *Life of Alexander*, 14). The fundamental principle of his philosophy was that happiness could be achieved only by satisfying one's natural needs in the easiest and cheapest way. Since this inevitably involved a certain shamelessness he was known as the 'Dog' (*Cyne*) and his followers as Cynics. No trace of his tomb has come to light.

Bellerophontes, the brave and beautiful, was the legendary grandson of Sisyphus (cf. p. 8 above); in his marvellous feats he was aided by the winged horse Pegasus. Cf. 3.5 and 4.1-2. Aphrodite Melaenis could also be translated Black or Dark Aphrodite. The origin of the title is unknown; elsewhere Pausanias explains that "the goddess has this title for no other reason than the fact that human copulations do not always take place in daylight like those of cattle but mostly at night" (8:6.5). On Laïs, a legendary beauty, see Plutarch, *Moralia,* 767F (p. 108 below). Since this part of the city has not been excavated it is impossible to say which, if any, of these edifices were in existence at the time of Paul.

The Corinthian Agora

2.6 The things worthy of mention in the city include the extant remains of antiquity, but the greater number of them belong to the period of its second ascendancy.

On the market-place (agora), where most of the sanctuaries are, stand Artemis surnamed Ephesian and wooden images of Dionysus, which are covered with gold with the exception of their faces; these are ornamented with red paint.

2.7 They are called Lysius and Bacchaeüs, and I too give the story told about them. They say that Pentheus treated Dionysus despitefully, his crowning outrage being that he went to Cithaeron, to spy upon the women, and climbing

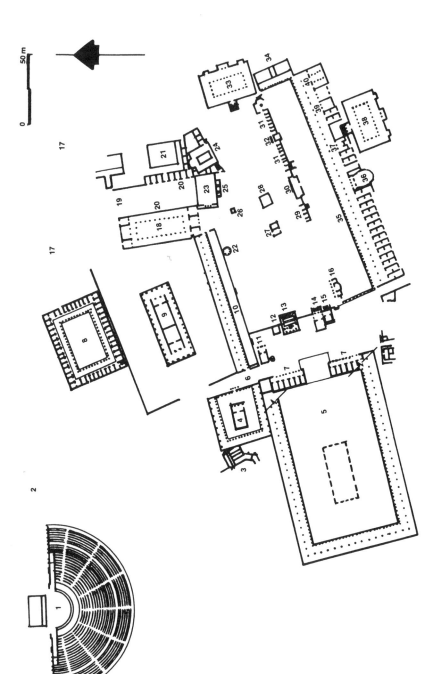

Fig. 5. The Agora at Corinth c. A.D. 50.
The buildings are dated by the reigns of the emperors Augustus
(31 B.C.-A.D. 14), Tiberius (A.D. 14-37), and Claudius (A.D. 41-
54). P = mentioned by Pausanias.

1. Theatre (Aug.). P
2. Erastus Pavement.
3. Well of Glauce. P
4. Temple of Hera Acraea (Aug.).
5. Temple. P
6. Road to Sicyon. P
7. Shops (Aug.).
8. North Market (Tib.).
9. Temple of Aethena. P
10. North-West Stoa (Aug.).
11. Temple of Tyche (Aug.) P
12. Babbius Monument (Tib.).
13. Fountain (Tib.). P
14. Temple of Apollo (Aug.). P
15. Temple of Aphrodite (Aug.). P
16. ?
17. Probable site of market.
18. Basilica (Aug.).
19. Lechaeum Road. P
20. Shops.

21. Market ?
22. Sacred Spring.
23. Ramp.
24. Peirene Fountain. P
25. Propylaea (Aug.).
26. Statue of Aethena. P
27. Altar.
28. Stone Platform.
29. Shops (Claud.).
30. Bema (Aug. or Claud.).
31. Shops (Claud.).
32. Artemis Ephesia ? P
33. Julian Basilica (Tib.).
34. Record Office ? (Tib.).
35. South Stoa (pre-146 B.C.).
36. City Council Chamber.
37. Fountain House.
38. South Basilica (Tib.).
39. Office of the Agonothetes.
40. Office of Hellanodikai.

up a tree beheld what was done. When the women detected Pentheus, they immediately dragged him down, and joined in tearing him, living as he was, limb from limb. Afterwards, as the Corinthians say, the Pythian priestess commanded them by an oracle to discover that tree and to worship it equally with the god. For this reason they have made these images from the tree.

2.8 There is also a temple of Fortune, with a standing image of Parian marble. Beside it is a sanctuary for all the gods. Hard by is built a fountain, on which is a bronze Poseidon; under the feet of Poseidon is a dolphin spouting water. There is also a bronze Apollo surnamed Clarius and a statue of Aphrodite made by Hermogenes of Cythera. There are two bronze, standing images of Hermes, for one of which a temple has been made. The images of Zeus also are in the open; one had not a surname, another they call Chthonius, and the third Most High.

3.1 In the middle of the market-place is a bronze Athena, on the pedestal of which are wrought in relief figures of the Muses. Above the market-place is a temple of Octavia the sister of Augustus, who was emperor of the Romans after Caesar, the founder of modern Corinth.

Coming from Craneum it would have been most natural for Pausanias to enter the agora through the South Stoa (n. 35 in fig. 5); apparently he then descended to the lower northern part by a staircase in the center or on the east (Wiseman, 1979:529). He would thus have surveyed the monuments in the agora in an anticlockwise direction.

According to Pausanias there were some remains from the pre-146 B.C. period — unfortunately he does not tell us which — but the greater part of what he saw was subsequent to 44 B.C. Regrettably he was uninterested in the fact that the city had undergone extensive reconstruction after the earthquake in A.D. 77 and that there was a massive building boom in the first half of the 2nd cent. A.D., because our interest lies in what would have been visible to Paul. We are fortunate, therefore, in being able to invoke the aid of archaeology. The results of almost 90 years of intensive investigation under the auspices of the American School of Classical Studies at Athens are consigned in a series of technical reports under the title *Corinth* (20 volumes to date). The essential conclusions are conveniently summarized by J. Wiseman (1979:509-528) in a study which has served as the main source for the commentary on the rest of Pausanias. If archaeology permits us to determine which edifices were in existence at the middle of the 1st cent. A.D. it is Pausanias who gives them names.

The map of Corinth in A.D. 50 in fig. 5 was drawn by Charles K. Williams II, Director of the Corinth excavations, and the bracketed numbers in the commentary refer to this plan. It will be immediately obvious that Pausanias does not mention all that was visible in the agora; his interest was above all drawn by what could be related to the ancient religion of the Greeks. Hence, in each section, I shall deal first with the edifices he mentions following his order, and then pass to those he omitted. In order not to overload the commentary I leave out of account the architectural elements which came into existence after the time of Paul. Buildings are dated by the reigning Roman emperor; the three in question here are Augustus (31 B.C. — A.D. 14), Tiberius (A.D. 14-37), and Claudius (A.D. 41-54).

Three statue bases were found in the tetrastyle building (n. 32) whose overhang would have offered protection for the two wooden statues of Dionysus which may have stood there in addition to that of Ephesian Artemis. Nothing either excludes or guarantees their existence at the time of Paul. Pausanias then moves to the north end of the west side of the agora, encountering first the temple of Fortune (n. 11), identified by the discovery in the vicinity of statues of Nike and Tyche; it was built under Augustus.

The fountain (n. 13) is attributed to Cn. Babbius Philinus, a Corinthian magistrate under both Augustus and Tiberius, because his name is inscribed on the base of the dolphin. Beside the fountain is a small monument (n. 12) consisting of a circle of Corinthian columns set on a square pedestal and surmounted by a concial roof terminating in a pine cone (Wiseman, 1979:518). Precisely the same inscription appeared *twice,* on the band above the columns and on the pedestal; it read:

> Gnaeus Babbius Philinus, aedile and pontifex, had this monument erected at his own expense, and he approved it in his official capacity as duovir (Kent: 73).

Babbius, obviously, was not prepared to take the chance that his successor might not agree with the projected monument! The absence of his father's name suggests that Babbius was a freedman, which goes some towards explaining his insecurity complex. This little exercise in self-recommendation (cf. 2 Cor 3:1) must have inspired some rather cynical reflections on the use of power, if it had not become a standing joke in the city as a symbol of the deplorable taste of noveau riche freedmen, which would explain why Pausanias passes over it in silence.

Pausanias' language implies that the statues of Clarian Apollo and of Aphrodite were under cover. Thus, they must have been housed in the two small temples, Apollo in n. 14 and Aphrodite in n. 15 which in addition had a dedication to Venus on its tympanum. Both are dated to the time of Augustus. In the middle of the lower part of the agora a round drum stood on a stepped base (n. 26); it certainly carried a colossal bronze statue, perhaps the Athena mentioned by Pausanias. The east facade of the temple of Octavia (n. 5) was constructed under Augustus, but the building within only some time later, perhaps under Claudius.

Other aspects of the agora Pausanias considered unworthy of notice. After all, they were commonplace to a man of his age; they were similar in every city he knew. Yet precisely because they were so ordinary they were integral to the life of every Corinthian. He does not, for example, mention the basement restaurant or tavern located just off the south-west corner of the agora. Damaged by an earthquake in A.D. 22/23, it was fortunately repaired because it provides a most graphic illustration of the cosmopolitan character of the city in Paul's time. It used pottery from Asia Minor, Syria, the islands of the Aegean, Rome and southern Italy (Wright).

The South Stoa (n. 35) was a survival from the pre-146 B.C. city. Then it had been lined by shops, but before the end of the reign of Augustus those at the east end had begun to be converted into administrative offices. Archaeologists have identified the Council Chamber (n. 36) from which the Roman city was run, the Fountain House (n. 37), a cool place to congregate, the office of the president of the Isthmian games (n. 39), and nearby the room used by the ten judges of the games (n. 40). Its structure and its proximity to the administrative center suggest that n. 34 may have been the Record Office (tax returns, land registration, etc.). The twin basilicas (nn. 33 and 38) were erected under Tiberius and would have been suitable for the display and selling of a variety of goods.

The agora was divided into two levels by a line of structures parallel to the South Stoa. The bema (Acts 18:12 — cf. p. 149 below), or speaker's platform (n. 30), stood in the center; it is dated to A.D. 44 but could be as early as the reign of Augustus. From here public proclamations were read, and here the magistrates sat; those who appeared before them stood on the square stone platform (n. 28) just beside the altar (n. 27). The bema was flanked by a series of shops (nn. 29 and 31); those to the east are certainly prior to A.D. 50, but the date of those on the west (n. 29) is under discussion. The function of two other structures (nn. 16 and 32) is unknown. The other side of the agora was limited by the Northwest Stoa (n. 10) built during the reign of Augustus. Just in front was the Sacred Spring (n. 22).

On the Road to Lechaeum

3.2   On leaving the market-place (agora) along the road to Lechaeum you come to a gateway, on which are two gilden chariots, one carrying Phaëthon the son of Helius (*Sun*), the other Helius himself. A little farther away from the gateway, on the right as you go in, is a bronze Heracles.

3.3   After this is the entrance to the water of Peirene. The legend about Peirene is that she was a woman who became a spring because of her tears shed in lamentation for her son Cenchrias, who was unintentionally killed by Artemis. The spring is ornamented with white marble, and there have been made chambers like caves, out of which the water flows into an open-air well. It is pleasant to drink, and they say that the Corinthian bronze, when red-hot is tempered by this water, since bronze...the Corinthians have not.

Moreover near Peirene are an image and a sacred enclosure of Apollo; in the latter is a painting of the exploit of Odysseus against the suitors.

3.4   Proceeding on the direct road to Lechaeum we see a bronze image of a seated Hermes. By him stands a ram, for Hermes is the god who is thought most to care for and to increase flocks, as Homer puts it in the *Iliad* (14:490): "Son was he of Phorbas, the dearest of Trojans to Hermes, rich in flocks, for the god vouchsafed him wealth in abundance." The story told at the mysteries of the Mother about Hermes and the ram I know but do not tell. After the image of Hermes come Poseidon, Leucothea, and Palaemon on a dolphin.

3.5   The Corinthians have baths in many parts of the city, some put up at public expense and one by the emperor Hadrian. The most famous of them is near the Poseidon. It was made by the Spartan Eurycles, who beautified it with various kinds of stone, especially the one quarried at Croceae in Laconia. On the left of the entrance stands a Poseidon, and after him Artemis hunting.

Throughout the city are many fountains, for the Corinthians have a copious supply of flowing water, besides the water which the emperor Hadrian brought from Lake Stymphalus, but the most noteworthy is the one by the side of the image of Artemis. Over it is a Bellerophontes, and the water flows through the hoof of the horse Pegasus.

The road to the port at Lechaeum (cf. p. 19 above) started from the northeast side of the agora (cf. fig. 5). The monumental gateway described by Pausanias was erected only in the last decades of the 1st cent. A.D. However, there is evidence to show that in the time of Augustus there had been a gateway (n. 25) with a large central arch flanked by two smaller arches. From it one descended by a ramp (n. 23) to the unpaved Lechaeum Road (n. 19).

The Spring of Peirene (n. 24) that Paul knew was very different from the one described by Pausanias because it had undergone extensive modifications at least twice in the interval. In the time of Augustus a two-story screen wall with an apse on the north surrounded a rectangular sunken area; water could be drawn from at least 15 spouts.

Corinthian bronze was famous and will be dealt with more fully on p. 86 below. The formulation of Pausanias implies that it was still being manufactured in the 2nd cent. A.D.; see also Plutarch (p. 103 below) but see Petronius (p. 83 below). That it was tempered in this particular fountain, despite the availability of water elsewhere (3.5), would seem to suggest that the water made a specific contribution to its unique character. It has been noted that the water of Peirene leaves an ochre-like deposit, and this has given rise to the hypothesis that it lent colour to the bronze (Frazer: 24). Pausanias does not say that the bronze was tempered in the spring itself. There may have been a foundry in the vicinity. There certainly was in the early days of the colony: "A bronze smithy, including an oven for heating, a bench for working the metal, and channels supplied with water from Peirene, is located east of the Lechaeum Road below the Peribolus of Apollo" (Wiseman, 1979:512). This establishment must have moved elsewhere in the vicinity when the colonnades and shops of the courtyard of Apollo (n. 21) were erected in the days of Augustus. This edifice was remodelled in the 2nd cent. A.D.

Unfortunately there is a break in the text of Pausanias just at the point where he claims that something was not found at Corinth. It has been suggested that the reference is to copper and tin, the raw materials of bronze, because there are no ancient mines or slag heaps in the neighbourhood of the city (Frazer: 25). On the sources of copper, cf. Pliny, *Natural History*, 34:2.

What Pausanias says about the number of baths is not at all surprising; they functioned as community centers in all Roman cities. A large bathing establishment has been partially excavated between nn. 17 and 21. It may be the one attributed to Eurycles. It underwent radical remodelling in the 2nd cent. A.D. and so the Eurycles in question may be Eurycles Herculanus, who was active in the reigns of Trajan (A.D. 98-117) and Hadrian (A.D. 117-138), rather than C. Junius Eurycles who was influential at Corinth during the days of Augustus (Kent: 125), and who made much mischief between Herod the Great and his sons (Josephus, *Antiquities*, 16:300-310; *Jewish War*, 1:513-533.). Thus what Paul might have seen there is dubious.

Unfortunately no study has been done on the water resources of ancient Corinth. This would have been of great assistance in establishing an estimate of the population (Wilkinson), since the extensive un-built areas do not permit us to derive figures based on analogies with population density elsewhere (Broshi). In fact, no hypothesis regarding the number of inhabitants of Roman Corinth has been put forward (Wiseman, 1978:12).

It is difficult to say whether the aqueduct built by Hadrian (A.D. 117-138) was required by an increase in the population, or whether it was designed to offset the summer drop in water supplies. Lake Stymphalus lies some 40 kms west-southwest of Corinth, and Pausanias (8:22.3) mentions a significant decrease in its summer flow. In addition to the springs, the Corinthians relied on wells and cisterns, but Wiseman notes that "It is still a rare summer in the Corinthia when the majority of the wells do not run dry." (1978:10).

Pausanias does not mention the shops (n. 20) which lined both sides of the Lechaeum Road. On the west side 16 shops vaulted with masonry supported the east side of a large basilica (n. 18). Built in the last quarter of the 1st cent. B.C., it may have served as a law court.

Further out along the Lechaeum Road were food markets (n. 17). The one to the west is dated to the late 1st or early 2nd cent. A.D. (Wiseman, 1979:526), but since the pre-146 B.C. agora was located in this area (Wiseman, 1979:489) it is likely that there was a market in the vicinity, and that it continued to serve the squatters in the ruins (cf. Cicero, p. 46 below). It is not impossible that a very badly broken inscription, whose thirteen fragments were found in various places, testifies to the restoration of such a market in the time of Augustus: "Quintus Cornelius Secundus, son of [_____] of the tribe Aemilia, and his wife Maecia, daughter of [Quintus], his son [_____ Cornelius Secundus] Maecianus, his son Quintus Secundus, his [daughter] Cornelia [Secunda, who is the wife of Quintus] Maecius Cleogenes the freedman of Quintus (Maecius) [built?] the meatmarket [_____] along with [_____] and a fishmarket [_____]. (Kent: 127). The word for meatmarket is *macellum*, which in Greek dress is the term used by Paul when he advises those who had scruples about eating meat offered to idols "Eat whatever is sold in the meatmarket (*en makellôi*) without raising any question on the grounds of conscience" (1 Cor 10:25; cf. Cadbury). Most of the meat generally available seems to have originated as sacrificial offerings (Smith: 12). In consequence, fish was specially prized, and a tremendous variety could be obtained (Athenaeus, *Deipnosophistae,* 281-330).

On the Road to Sicyon

3.6   As you go along another road from the marketplace (agora), which leads to Sicyon, you can see on the right of the road a temple and a bronze image of Apollo, and a little further on a well called the Well of Glauce. Into this, they say, she threw herself in the belief that the water would be a cure for the drugs of Medea. Above this well has been built what is called the Odeum, beside which is the tomb of Medea's children. Their names were Mermerus and Pheres, and they are said to have been stoned to death by the Corinthians owing to the gifts which legend says they brought to Glauce.

3.7   But as their death was violent and illegal, the young babies of the Corinthians were destroyed by them until, at the command of the oracle, yearly sacrifices were established in their honour and a figure of Terror set up. This figure still exists, being the likeness of a woman frightful to look at; but after Corinth was laid waste by the Romans and the old Corinthians wiped out, the new settlers broke the custom of offering those sacrifices to the sons of Medea, nor do their children cut their hair for them or wear black clothes.

3.8-11   (Mixed-up myth of the murderous misfortunes of Medea ending with the words:) For these reasons Medea too departed and handed over the kingdom to Sisyphus.

4.1   This is the account that I read, and not far from the tomb is the temple of Athena Chalinitis (*Bridler*). For Athena, they say, was the divinity who gave most help to Bellerophontes, and she delivered to him Pegasus, having herself broken in and bridled him. The image of her is wood, but face, hands and feet are of white marble.

The Sicyon Road (n. 6) ran north from the west side of the agora. The temple on the right can only be the Archaic Temple (n. 9). Dating from the 6th cent. B.C. this sanctuary had been restored by the Romans by the early part of the 1st cent. A.D., the area around the temple being paved with limestone slabs. Its dedication to Apollo is based almost exclusively on the account of Pausanias, which is not as precise as one might wish. There are indications, however, that it may in fact have been dedicated to Athena.

Pausanias next mentions the Well of Glauce (n. 3), even though he would have had to turn the corner of the temple of Hera Acraea (n. 4) to see it. The temple was certainly in existence at the time of Paul, but the precinct walls may be later. This omission was probably due to an oversight.

Though not as distinguished as the Spring of Peirene (n. 24), the Well of Glauce was just as old. When Jason, the leader of the mythological Argonauts, abandoned Medea for Glauce, the former slew her rival by sending her a dress impregnated with drugs which burst into flames as soon as Glauce put it on. In response the Corinthians killed Medea's children who had brought the gift, but were eventually forced to find some means of warding off the vengeance of the innocent victims. Thus, according to the Scholiast on Euripides, *Medea,* 273, "Seven boys and seven girls of the most distinguished families spend a year in the sanctuary of the goddess, and with sacrifices appease the anger of the murdered children, and the wrath which their murder excited in the breast of the goddess." Presumably these were the children who, according to Pausanias, used to cut their hair and wear black clothing (Frazer: 27). This rite was abandoned by the Roman colonists, but the persistence of the statue of Terror would appear to indicate that the legend of Glauce's horrible fate had remained attached to the well.

The Odeum, or music hall, did not exist at the time of Paul. It was first built in the late 1st cent. A.D. and thoroughly remodelled and roofed by Herodes the Athenian (cf. 1.8 above) in the 2nd cent. A.D. The temple of Athena Chalinitis has not been found.

The Early History of Corinth

4.2   That Bellerophontes was not an absolute king, but was subject to Proetus and the Argives is the belief of myself and of all who have read carefully the Homeric poems. When Bellerophontes migrated to Lycia it is clear that the Corinthians none the less were subject to the despots of Argos or Mycenae. By themselves they provided no leader for the campaign against Troy but shared in the expedition as part of the forces, Mycenaean and other, led by Agamemnon.

4.3   Sisyphus had other sons besides Glaucus, the father of Bellerophontes; a second was Ornytion, and besides him there were Thersander and Almus. Ornytion had a son Phocus, reputed to have been begotten by Poseidon. He migrated to Tithorea in what is now called Phocis, but Thoas, the younger son of Ornytion, remained behind at Corinth. Thoas begat Damophon, Damophon begat Propodas, and Propodas begat Doridas and Hyanthidas.

While these were reigning the Dorians took the field against Corinth, their leader being Aletes, the son of Hippotas, the son of Phylas, the son of Antiochus, the son of Heracles. So Doridas and Hyanthidas gave up the kingship to Aletes and remained at Corinth, but the Corinthians were conquered in battle and expelled by the Dorians.

4.4   Aletes himself and his descendants reigned for five generations to Baccis, the son of Prumnis, and, named after him, the Bacchidae reigned for five more generations to Telestes, the son of Aristodemus.

Telestes was killed in hate by Arieus and Perantas, and there were no more kings, but presidents taken from the Bacchidea and ruling for one year, until Cypselus, the son of Eetion, became tyrant and expelled the Bacchidae.

Cypselus was a descendant of Melas, the son of Antasus. Melas from Gonussa above Sicyon joined the Dorians in the expedition against Corinth. When the god expressed disapproval, Aletes at first ordered Melas to withdraw to another place in Greece, but afterwards, mistaking the oracle, he received him as a settler.

Such I found to be the history of the Corinthian kings.

This excursus moves almost imperceptibly from mythology into genuine history. The Dorians from northern Greece settled in the Peloponnese about 1000 B.C. ending the splendid era of Mycenae. One of their families, the Bacchidae, ruled Corinth from the mid-9th to the mid-7th cent. B.C. They founded the colonies of Corcyra (modern Corfu) and Syracuse, and developed ceramics and shipbuilding. About 655 B.C. they were supplanted by Cypselus, the history of whose house is carried on by Strabo (cf. p. 56 below).

On the Road to Sicyon (cont.)

4.5   Now the sanctuary of Athena Chalinitis is by their theatre, and near is a naked wooden image of Heracles, said to be a work of Daedalus. All the works of this artist, although rather uncouth to look at, are nevertheless distinguished by a kind of inspiration. Above the theatre is a sanctuary of Zeus surnamed in the latin tongue Capitolinus, which might be rendered into Greek *Coryphaeos.*

Not far from this theatre is the ancient gymnasium, and a spring called Lerna. Pillars stand around it, and seats have been made to refresh in summer time those who have entered it. By this gymnasium are temples of Zeus and Asclepius. The images of Asclepius and of Health are of white marble, that of Zeus is of bronze.

The theatre (n. 1) was built in the last years of the 5th cent. B.C. but had been repaired by the Romans late in the reign of Augustus or early in that of Tiberius when a multi-storeyed stage wall of stuccoed porous stone was added. Thus it would have been a functioning institution at the time of Paul, and would have held about 14,000 persons.

Daedalus was a mythological figure symbolic of superlative craftsmanship, and the attribution to him of a statue, in this case Heracles, means only that it was considered to be of great antiquity. A wooden statue would have had little attraction for the looters of 146 B.C. and 44 B.C. (cf. Strabo, p. 66 below) and so it may have been one of the survivors of pre-Roman Corinth.

The title of the temple of Zeus Capitolinus indicates that it was constructed after the founding of the Roman colony in 44 B.C. but exactly when cannot be determined because the area has not been excavated.

In keeping with his usual practice Pausanias does not mention a large market area (n. 8). Constructed in the first half of the 1st cent. A.D. it consisted of a large courtyard surrounded by a Doric colonnade behind which was a row of shops (cf. p. 177 below). There were entrances on the east and west.

Between the market (n. 8) and the theatre (n. 1) and on the level of the stage of the latter was an area paved with gray Acrocorinthian limestone (n. 2). This is of unusual interest because of an inscription. Only the cuttings for the letters remain, the bronze contents having been ripped out by looters. It reads [_____] *Erastus pro aedilit*[*at*]*e s*(*ua*) *p(ecunia) stravit.* "[_____] Erastus in return for his aedileship laid (the pavement) at his own expense." (Kent: 99). Since the pavement was laid before the middle of the 1st cent. A.D. this individual is identified with the Erastus who was city treasurer at the time of Paul and a Christian (Rom 16:23).

The next complex mentioned by Pausanias is located some 400 meters due north of the theatre and just inside the city wall (cf. fig. 4). The origin of the name Lerna is obscure; an association with the nine-headed Lernaian Hydra (Water Serpent) has been suggested (Lang: 3). At least by the time of Tiberius a 2 meter deep swimming pool stood in the middle of a courtyard walled on three sides; on the fourth were passages into three underground chambers. It was served by the same water supply as the temple of Asclepius some 150 meters to the north-east. This sanctuary existed in the pre-146 B.C. period, but was brought back into use early in the history of the Roman colony; for more detail cf. p. 170 below. The gymnasium mentioned by Pausanias did not exist at the time of Paul; it was erected at the end of the 1st cent. or the beginning of the 2nd cent. A.D.

The gate by which the Sicyon Road left the city has not been discovered but traces of the road outside, which continued to serve until the late 4th cent. A.D., indicate that it must have been roughly where it is positioned in fig. 4 (Wiseman, 1978:84).

On the Road to Acrocorinth

4.6   Acrocorinth is a mountain above the city, assigned to Helius by Briareos when he acted as adjudicator, and handed over, the Corinthians say, by Helius to Aphrodite.

As you go up to Acrocorinth you see two precincts of Isis, one of Isis surnamed Pelagian, and the other of Egyptian Isis, and two sanctuaries of Serapis, one of them being of Serapis called 'in Canopus.'

4.7   After these are altars to Helius, and a sanctuary of Necessity and Force, into which it is not customary to enter. Above it are a temple of the Mother of the gods and a throne; the image and the throne are made of stone.

The temple of the Fates and that of Demeter and the Maid have images that are not exposed to view. Here too is the temple of Hera Bunaea set up by Bunus the son of Hermes. It is for this reason that the goddess is called Bunaea.

From time immemorial Acrocorinth was the citadel of Corinth. A rugged crag of grey limestone 575 meters high, it is precipitous on all sides. Access is feasible only on the west where a saddle connects Acrocorinth to the lower eminence of Penteskouphia. The road from the agora must have zigzagged up the slope which becomes progressively steeper; the ancient and modern lines are certainly different (Wiseman, 1979:469). Of the sanctuaries mentioned by Pausanias only that of Demeter and the Maid has been excavated. This sanctuary was brought back into use, if it was ever completely abandoned, in the early days of the Roman colony, because Demeter was the goddess who governed the fruits of the earth, and one of the first things the settlers had to do was to ensure a good food supply.

The Summit of Acrocorinth

5.1   On the summit of Acrocorinth is a temple of Aphrodite. The images are Aphrodite armed, Helius, and Eros with a bow. The spring, which is behind the temple, they say was the gift of Asopus to Sisyphus.

The latter knew, so runs the legend, that Zeus had ravished Aegina, the daughter of Asopus, but refused to give information to the seeker before he had a spring given him on Acrocorinth. When Asopus granted this request Sisyphus turned informer, and on this account he receives — if anyone believes the story — punishment in Hades. I have heard it said that this spring and Peirene are the same, the water in the city flowing hence underground.

5.2   This Asopus rises in the Phliasian territory, flows through the Sicyonian, and empties itself into the sea here. His daughters, say the Phliasians, were Corcyra, Aegina, and Thebe. Corcyra and Aegina gave new names to the islands called Scheria and Oenone, while from Thebe is named the city below the Cadmea. The Thebans do not agree, but say that Thebe was the daughter of the Boeotian, and not of the Phliasian, Asopus. The other stories about the river are current among both the Phliasians and the Sicyonians, for instance that its water is foreign and not native, in that the Maeander, descending from Celaenae through Phrygia and Caria, and emptying itself into the sea at Miletus, goes to the Peloponnesus and forms the Asopus. I remember hearing a similar story from the Delians, that the stream which they call Inopus comes to them from the Nile. Such is the account I heard of the Asopus.

The two edifices on Acrocorinth mentioned by Pausanias are also the only ones recorded by Strabo (cf. p. 59 below). The temple of Aphrodite stood on the higher eastern peak; due south of it (thus 'behind' with respect to the city) the spring of Upper Peirene burst forth near the edge of the cliff (cf. fig. 4). Nothing remains of the former except some cuttings in the rock. The vault over the spring is dated to the 3rd cent. B.C. Since Pausanias notes the association of the spring with Sisyphus, his silence regarding the Sisypheium mentioned by Strabo is significant; it was probably not rebuilt in the Roman period. Strabo (p. 59 below) may have been the source of the idea that Upper and Lower Peirene were linked.

The Asopus is a major river to the west of Corinth which enters the Gulf of Corinth near Sicyon (cf. fig. 1). The legend that it was an extension of the Maeander flowing beneath the sea from near Miletus (Acts 20:17) is intriguing in view of the close relationship between the Christian communities at Ephesus and Corinth (1 Cor 1:11).

Outside Corinth

5.4   When you have turned from Acrocorinth into the mountain road you see the Teneatic Gate and a sanctuary of Eilethyia. The town called Tenea is just about sixty stades distant. The inhabitants say that they are Trojans who were taken prisoners in Tenedos by the Greeks, and were permitted by Agamemnon to dwell in their present home. For this reason they honour Apollo more than any other god.

5.5 As you go from Corinth, not into the interior but along the road to Sicyon, there is on the left not far from the city a burnt temple. There have, of course, been many wars carried on in Corinthian territory, and naturally houses and sanctuaries outside the wall have been fired. But this temple, they say, was Apollo's, and Pyrrhus the son of Achilles burned it down. Subsequently I heard another account, that the Corinthians built the temple for Olympian Zeus, and that suddenly fire from some quarter fell on it and destroyed it.

The Teneatic Gate can only be on the saddle between Acrocorinth and Penteskouphia (cf. fig. 4), but no trace of wall, gate or sanctuary has been discovered (Wiseman, 1978:81). The Teneans' conception of their origin is highly indicative of the power and persistence of legend, a factor that should not be lost sight of when evaluating the impact on the population of the mythological associations so sedulously collected by Pausanias.

Pausanias' mention of houses outside the wall is confirmed by the existence of a 2nd cent. A.D. Roman villa not far beyond the Sicyonian Gate (Wiseman, 1979:528). How many others there were, and of what date, cannot be estimated.

Elsewhere in his work Pausanias makes a number of passing references to Corinth, some of which are important from different points of view.

DESCRIPTION OF GREECE, 5:1.2

The Arcadians have from the beginning to the present time continued in possession of their own country. The rest of the Peloponnese belongs to immigrants. The modern Corinthians are the latest inhabitants of the Peloponnese, and from my time to the time when they received their land from the Roman emperor is 217 years.

The importance of this passage is that it provides a *terminus ante quem* for Pausanias' visit to Corinth. If Julius Caesar sent settlers to Corinth in 44 B.C. (cf. Appian, p. 117 below), Pausanias must have been writing this paragraph in A.D. 174.

DESCRIPTION OF GREECE, 5:25.1

I have enumerated the images of Zeus within the Altis with the greatest accuracy. For the offering near the great temple, though supposed to be a likeness of Zeus, is really Alexander, the son of Philip. It was set up by a Corinthian, not one of the old Corinthians, but one of those settlers whom the emperor planted in the city.

Altis was the sacred grove of Zeus (5:10.1), the center of the great sanctuary in which the Olympic games were celebrated. Many foreigners made offerings, e.g. Antiochus IV Ephiphanes (5:12.4) may have presented the veil looted from the temple in Jerusalem (Levi: 2/231), so that the gift of a Roman colonist of Corinth is significant only as an indicator of the growing wealth of the colony. Pausanias would have spoken rather differently had the donor been a Greek. Nothing is known about the statue in question.

DESCRIPTION OF GREECE, 7:16.7-10

16.7 As soon as night fell, the Achaeans who had escaped to Corinth after the battle fled from the city, and there fled with them most of the Corinthians themselves. At first Mummius hesitated to enter Corinth, although the gates were open, as he suspected that an ambush had been laid within the walls. But on the third day after the

battle he proceeded to storm Corinth and to set it on fire.
16.8   The majority of those found in it were put to the sword by the Romans, but the women and children Mummius sold into slavery. He also sold all the slaves who had been set free, had fought on the side of the Achaeans, and had not fallen at once on the field of battle. The most admired votive offerings and works of art were carried off by Mummius; those of less account he gave to Philopoemen, the general sent by Attalus; even in my day there were Corinthian spoils at Pergamum.
16.9   The walls of all the cities that had made war against Rome Mummius demolished, disarming the inhabitants, even before assistant commissioners were despatched from Rome, and when these did arrive, he proceeded to put down democracies and to establish governments based on property qualification. Tribute was imposed on Greece, and those with property were forbidden to acquire possessions in a foreign country....
16.10   .... Although the Romans granted the Greeks remission of these payments, yet down to my day a Roman governor has been sent to the country. The Romans call him the Governor, not of Greece, but of Achaia, because the cause of the subjection of Greece was the Achaeans, at that time the head of the Greek nation.

This text forms the conclusion to a detailed history of the Achaean League (7:7.1-16.10) which Pausanias introduces into his description of Achaia. It is the most complete record of what happened to the inhabitants when the city fell in 146 B.C. (cf. Dio Cassius, p. 128 below), but further references to the looting are to be found in Strabo (p. 66 below).

It is clear that the city was denuded of population. Many had fled, and of those that remained Mummius executed the adult males, both slaves and free, and sold the rest into slavery. Plutarch, however, notes with pride one exception. "Best of all was the young Corinthian prisoner of war, when his city was destroyed, and Mummius was reviewing such free-born boys as could read and write, ordered him to write down a line of verse, he wrote, 'O thrice and four times happy Greeks who perished then.' (Homer, *Odyssey*, 5:306). It is said that Mummius was affected to the point of tears and let all the boy's relations go free." (*Moralia,* 737A).

It is difficult to estimate the extent of the devastation. Fire would not have rendered completely uninhabitable a city built mostly of stone, an assumption that has been confirmed by the excavations (Wiseman, 1979:494). It seems very probable that at least some of those who fled returned to the city once the Roman army had departed (but cf. Dio Cassius, p. 128 below). In fact, for the period 146-44 B.C., there is evidence of the use of places of cult, building activities, and trade (Wiseman, 1979:495); cf. also Cicero (p. 46 below). Thus, at Corinth there was a definite continuity between the Greek and Roman periods. Unfortunately it is impossible to estimate the impact this might have had on the colonists of 44 B.C. The inhabitants they found would immediately have assumed a very low position on the social scale, but the memories and traditions that they preserved would surely have had increasing influence as the colony progressively discovered its own identity.

What Pausanias says regarding the reorganisation of Greece in the post-146 B.C. period is full of wild generalisations; what he says is true only of certain places at some times (for details, cf. Larsen: 306-309). In particular, Pausanias is guilty of anachronism in speaking of control being exercised through the Governor of Achaia. Until the province of Achaia was established in 27 B.C. the supreme Roman authority in Greece was the Governor of Macedonia.

ANTIPATER OF SIDON

Nothing is known of this figure, who lived in the early second century B.C., beyond the somewhat enigmatic characterization by Meleager (c. 140-70 B.C.), "the cock signifies that he was a man who made himself heard, a champion too I suppose in love matters and a versatile songster. The sceptre he holds is emblematic of his speech and the die cast wide means that in his cups he fell and died.'' (*Greek Anthology,* 7:428).

GREEK ANTHOLOGY, 9:151

> Where is thy celebrated beauty, Doric Corinth?
> Where are the battlements of thy towers and your ancient wealth?
> Where are the temples of the immortals, the houses of the matrons of the town of Sisyphus, and her myriads of people? Not even a trace is left of thee, most unhappy of towns, but war has seized on and devoured everything. We alone, the Nereids, Ocean's daughters, remain inviolate, and lament, like halcyons, thy sorrows.

The total destruction of Corinth by Mummius in 146 B.C. is clearly implied. Only the seas that wash the Isthmus it once controlled remain untouched. However, the form lends itself to rhetorical exaggeration, and a different picture emerges from eyewitnesses (see Cicero).

GREEK ANTHOLOGY, 7:493

> I, Rhodope, and my mother Boisca neither died of sickness, nor fell by the sword of the foes, but ourselves, when dreadful Ares burn the city of Corinth our country, chose a brave death. My mother slew me with the slaughtering knife, nor did she, unhappy woman, spare her own life, but tied the noose around her neck; for it was better than slavery to die in freedom.

This epigram is also attributed to Antipater of Thessalonica, who lived at the very end of the first century B.C., but it is listed among the epigrams collected by Meleager, and harmonizes better with the period prior to the foundation of the Roman colony; contrast Crinagoras below. It is the counterpart of the first epigram: once Corinth had gone who would wish to live?

POLYSTRATUS

Again, nothing is known of this epigrammatist beyond the fact that he was included in the first great critical anthology of epigrams by Meleager (c. 140-70 B.C.), who names him in conjunction with Antipater of Sidon (*Greek Anthology,* 4:1.4).

GREEK ANTHOLOGY 7:297

> Lucius has smitten sore the great Achaean Acrocorinth, the star of Hellas, and the twin parallel shores of the Isthmus. One heap of stones covers the bones of those slain in the rout; and the sons of Aeneas left unwept and unhallowed by funeral rites the Achaeans who burnt the house of Priam.

Lucius Mummius was the Roman general who sacked Corinth in 146 B.C. The Homeric allusions give a new dimension to the tragedy. Aeneas was a Trojan leader descended from the junior branch of the royal house headed by King Priam. According to legend, he fled from the burning city and became the founder of Rome. Thus it was his descendants who took long-awaited vengeance on the Greeks for their destruction of Troy.

CICERO

Born on 3 January 106 B.C. Marcus Tullius Cicero first appeared for the defense in a major trial in 80 B.C. He soon established himself as one of the leading lawyers in Rome. He also played a prominent role in public life, becoming praetor in 66 B.C., consul in 63 B.C., and proconsul of Cilicia in 51 B.C. A firm defender of the constitution, he was exiled for his opposition to the Triumvirate of Julius Caesar, Crassus, and Pompey. Permitted to return after a year, he became friendly with Caesar and Pompey but accepted no public appointments until forced to do so in 51 B.C. He had no part in the assassination of Caesar, but approved the action once convinced that the latter would not have governed constitutionally. In a series of brilliant speeches he stiffened the Senate's opposition to Mark Anthony, thereby incurring his undying hatred. Octavian assumed control in Rome in 43 B.C. and, in order to retain the support of Mark Anthony, sacrificed Cicero who was executed on 7 December of that year.

Cicero published voluminously, speeches both for the prosecution and for the defense, philosophical works, and personal letters. His precision and clarity ensured that his formulations became *the* model of Latin style for over 1000 years. Even still to say that someone speaks or writes Ciceronian Latin is the supreme compliment.

TUSCULAN DISPUTATIONS, 3:53:

> I have seen too in the Peloponnese in my youthful days some natives of Corinth who were slaves. All of them could have made the same lament as that in *Andromacha* "All this did I see...," but by the time I saw them they had ceased, it may be, to chant dirges. Their features, speech, all the rest of their movements and postures would have led one to say they were freemen of Argos or Sicyon; and at Corinth the sudden sight of the ruins had more effect upon me than upon the actual inhabitants, for long contemplation had had the hardening effect of length of time upon their souls.

A skilled translator and adaptor, one of Cicero's ambitions was to make Greek philosophy available to a Latin audience. He had the leisure to do so in the sad years of his opposition to the Triumvirate, and the form he chose was a series of dialogues set in his villa at Tusculum. The *Tusculum Disputations* were written in 45 B.C.

According to this text Cicero had actually visited Corinth. It must have been in the years 79-77 B.C. when, for reasons of health, he travelled in the East and attended the lectures of notable scholars in Athens and Rhodes. He thus saw the city in the dark period between its destruction in 146 B.C. and its restoration as a Roman colony in 44 B.C., and is the sole eyewitness to the fact that the ruins were not completely deserted, as is commonly supposed. Civic life would naturally have broken down completely, but it would be completely abnormal if those who had fled the city before the arrival of Mummius (cf. Pausanias, p. 43 above) had not returned when the opportunity offered. Set in the midst of an immensely fertile area (cf. below) Corinth had served as the principal market, and probably continued to serve as an exchange-center though on a greatly reduced scale.

ON THE AGRARIAN LAW

> They propose to sell...the rich and most fertile land of Corinth which, under the happy command of L. Mummius, had been added to the domain of the Roman people. (1:5).

> He puts up for auction the rich and fertile fields of Corinth. (2:51).

> In the whole world there are only three cities capable of sustaining the name and dignity of empire, Carthage, Corinth, and Capua. Carthage was destroyed because, with its multitude of men, and especially its natural situation — its ring of ports and armour of walls — it seemed to thrust itself out from Africa ready to spring on the two most productive islands of the Roman people. Scarcely a trace remains of Corinth. Placed in the narrowest part of Greece, as in a pass, it held on the land side the keys of the country and on the other side almost united, so narrow was the space between them, two seas open to navigation in diametrically opposed senses. Our ancestors were not content merely to take these far-distant cities, but completely destroyed them lest reviving they should one day reestablish themselves. (2:87).

These two discourses were spoken during the consulship of Cicero in 63 B.C. in opposition to an agrarian reform bill proposed by P. Sergius Rullus; they are sometimes entitled *Against Rullus*. One provision of this law was that land outside Italy which belonged to the state by right of conquest (the case of Corinth) should be sold or rented and the revenues used to buy up land in Italy for distribution to the vast urban proletariat. The idea was that they should become productive workers rather than recipients of the grain-dole. Cicero was opposed, not to the idea itself, but to the unlimited powers to be conferred on the commission of ten charged with the implementation of the law.

Cicero would have known the quality of the land in the Corinthia from first-hand experience, and he was obviously struck by the tremendous natural advantages of the site of the city. His claim that Corinth had the potential to become a capital to rival Rome is perhaps extravagant, but elsewhere he calls it "the light of all Greece" (*Pro lege Manilia*, 5). It suited the purpose of his speech to underline the possible danger of a Corinth free to develop in its own way, but when it was convenient he could equally well argue the opposite view as the next citation shows.

ON THE REPUBLIC, 2:7-9

Maritime cities also suffer a certain corruption and degeneration of morals; for they receive a mixture of strange languages and customs, and import foreign ways as well as foreign merchandise, so that none of their ancestral institutions can possibly remain unchanged. Even their inhabitants do not cling to their dwelling places, but are constantly being tempted far from home by soaring hopes and dreams; and even when their bodies stay at home, their thoughts nevertheless fare abroad and go wandering. In fact, no other influence did more to bring about the final overthrow of Carthage and Corinth, though they had long been tottering, than this scattering and dispersion of their citizens, due to the fact that the lust for trafficking and sailing the seas had caused them to abandon agriculture and the pursuit of arms.

Many things too that cause ruin to states as being incitements to luxury are supplied by the sea, entering either by capture or import; and even the mere delightfulness of such a site brings in its train many an allurement to pleasure through either extravagance or indolence. And what I said of Corinth may perhaps be said with truth of the whole of Greece; for even the Peloponnesus is almost in its entire extent close to the sea. . . . But nevertheless with all these disadvantages they possess one great advantage — all the products of the world can be brought by water to the city in which you live, and your people in turn can convey or send whatever their own fields produce to any country they like.

The inspiration of Cicero's treatise on the ideal commonwealth and its statesmen, written between 54 and 51 B.C., was obviously Plato's *Republic.* The ideal was embodied in the Roman state, and this reference to Corinth occurs in the context of his justification of the divine wisdom displayed in the selection of the site of Rome. By locating it on a river some distance inland one had all the advantages of proximity to the sea but none of the disadvantages, e.g. a surprise boat-attack.

His description of Corinth must be based partly on its legendary reputation (cf. Strabo, p. 57 below) and partly on his own experience of the port cities of the eastern Mediterranean. It contains nothing specific, but this does not detract from the truth of the generalisation. It would be a mistake, however, to imagine that agriculture in the Corinthia had been completely abandoned, even though many would have been drawn to leave the land by the lure of a great commercial center. The same phenomenon certainly occurred when the city was refounded in 44 B.C.

Cicero is somewhat less than fair in the reasons he assigns for the fall of Corinth in 146 B.C. It had founded a number of colonies overseas, but the fact that 5000 citizens went to Syracuse in 342 B.C. witnesses less to the temptation of 'soaring hopes and dreams' than to the pressure of excess population (Wiseman, 1978:12). As regard Corinth's military prowess, the Romans had been working since 172 B.C. to break up the Achaean League to which Corinth belonged. In 146 B.C. the League made war with Rome inevitable by declaring war on Sparta. Three of its armies, to which Corinth certainly supplied troops, were defeated by Q. Caecilius Metellus coming from Macedonia. That left only 14,000 infantry and 600 cavalry, an army recruited from untrained slaves and citizens, to face Mummius' 23,000 infantry and 3,500 cavalry in defense of Corinth (Wiseman, 1979:462).

AGAINST VERRES II, 4:97-98

> 97. Scipio, that most excellent of men, offered to this sanctuary chased bronze breastplates and helmets of Corinthian workmanship, as well as tall ewers of the same material and artistry; they were inscribed with his name. . . . All these were stolen by Verres. . . .
> 98. Perhaps you are the only one to delight in Corinthian vases, to discern the alloy of their metal, to recognize the beauty of their lines. None of this Scipio knew, that man so learned and cultured. It took you, without any redeeming quality, without culture, talent, or learning, to have the taste and the judgement.

In 70 B.C. Cicero acted as prosecuting attorney when Gaius Verres was tried for his abuse of power during his governorship of Sicily. One of his crimes was to have stolen from the sanctuary of the Great Mother at Engyum objects of Corinthian bronze which had been dedicated by Scipio Africanus Major (236-184 B.C.). Verres escaped judgement by going into voluntary exile, and it is a curious irony of fate that both he and his accuser, Cicero, met their death at the hands of Antony in 43 B.C. for refusing to hand over to him some Corinthian bronze (cf. Pliny the Elder, p. 88 below).

That Cicero should single out Corinthian bronze objects is a clear indication of the estimation in which they were held; they were appreciated not only for the quality of the metal but also for the artistry of the workmanship. This passage is the only one to mention that armour was made of Corinthian bronze; by Pliny's standards they may not have been authentic (cf. p. 89 below). The 'great ewers', on the contrary, are parallel to objects described by Callixeinius of Rhodes (mid-2nd cent. B.C.), "two mixing-bowls of Corinthian workmanship, on stands; these had on the brim seated figures in beaten metal, very striking; and on the neck and around the bowl were figures in relief, carefully fashioned; the capacity of each was 80 gallons." (Athenaeus, *Deipnosophistae*, 199e). By Pliny's criteria these could be authentic.

CRINAGORAS

Crinagoras was born c. 70 B.C. in Mytilene, capital of the island of Lesbos. An undistinguished poet, he took part in an embassy to Julius Caesar at Rome in 45 B.C. He was present, therefore, when the final touches were being put on the plan to resettle Corinth.

GREEK ANTHOLOGY, 9:284

> What inhabitants, O luckless city, have you received, and in place of whom? Alas for the great calamity to Greece! Would, Corinth, that you be lower than the ground and more desert than the Libyan sands, rather than wholly abandoned to such a crowd of scoundrelly slaves, you should vex the bones of the ancient Bacchiadae.

This is much more a Greek's lament for glories past than an accurate report. The new colonists were for the most part freedmen (see Strabo, p. 67 below), but the author found it intolerable that they should now hold the place of free men in what was once the pride of Greece.

STRABO

Born in Amasia in Pontus in 64 or 63 B.C., Strabo was of mixed Greek and Asiatic blood. His ancestors included eminent generals and priests, and inherited wealth enabled him to dedicate his life to scholarship and travel. He passed through Corinth on his way to Rome in 44 B.C., but it is not clear whether the first Roman colonists had already arrived at that moment. While in Rome he studied under Tyrannion, an illustrious geographer, and it was perhaps he who directed Strabo's interest towards historical geography. He made several later journeys to Rome on one of which he again visited Corinth (*Geography*, 10:5.3). This was in 29 B.C. when he had an opportunity to see what had been achieved by the new colony. During the five years he lived in Alexandria (c. 25-20 B.C.) he made full use of the works of previous geographers conserved in the famous library. He considered himself to have travelled widely, but in fact he gives no evidence of the sort of systematic exploration that his chosen discipline demanded; he simply made good use of the opportunities to accompany others. His *Geography* was completed about 7 B.C., and slightly revised about A.D. 18 some three or four years before his death.

GEOGRAPHY, 1:3.11

But Eratosthenes is so simple that, although he is a mathematician, he will not even confirm the doctrine of Archimedes, who, in his treatise *On Floating Bodies* says that the surface of every liquid body at rest and in equilibrium is spherical, the sphere having the same centre as the earth — a doctrine that is accepted by every one who has studied mathematics at all.

And so, although Eratosthenes himself admits that the Mediterranean Sea is one continuous sea, yet he does not believe that it has been brought under a law of one continuous surface, even in places that lie close together. And as authorities for such an ignorant opinion as this he summons engineers, although the mathematicians have declared that engineering is a branch of mathematics.

For he says that Demetrius, too, attempted to cut through the Isthmus of Corinth in order to provide a passage for his fleets, but was prevented by the engineers, after they had taken measurements and reported to him that the sea in the Corinthian Gulf was higher than at Cenchreae, so that, if he should cut through the intervening land, the whole strait about Aegina, Aegina itself, and the neighbouring islands would be submerged, and the canal would not be useful, either.

Although he had met Archimedes (c. 287-212 B.C.) in Alexandria and was himself a first-class mathematician (he had calculated the circumference of the earth and the distance and magnitude of the sun and the moon), Eratosthenes (c. 275-194 B.C.) failed to appreciate the relevance of the former's theorem to the problem of cutting a canal through the Isthmus of Corinth which had been proposed by Demetrius I, Poliorcetes, of Macedonia (336-283 B.C.).

Like most old wive's tales, the belief in the difference of sea-levels in the Corinthian gulf and the Saronic Gulf, on which the port of Cenchreae is located (cf. fig. 1), was not at all disturbed by scientific theory. It is mentioned by Philostratus (c. A.D. 170-245) as the reason why the canal of Nero (cf. Suetonius, p. 110 below) was abandoned, "They began to dig the canal at Lechaeum, but they had not advanced more than about four stadia of continuous excavation, when Nero stopped the work of cutting it, some say because Egyptian men of science explained to him the nature of the seas, and declared that the sea above Lechaeum would flood and obliterate the island of Aegina, but others claim that Nero apprehended a revolution in the empire." (*Life of Apollonius of Tyana*, 4:24). The same type of objection was raised when the Suez Canal was first proposed.

GEOGRAPHY, 8:6.20-23

Wealthy Corinth

20a. Corinth is called 'wealthy' because of its commerce, since it is situated on the Isthmus and is master of two harbours, of which the one leads straight to Asia, and the other to Italy; and it makes easy the exchange of merchandise from both countries that are so far distant from each other.

And just as in early times the Strait of Sicily was not easy to navigate, so also the high seas, and particularly the sea beyond Maleae, on account of the contrary winds; and hence the proverb, "But when you double Maleae forget your home." At any rate, to land their cargoes here was a welcome alternative to the voyage to Maleae for merchants from both Italy and Asia.

And also the duties on what was exported by land from the Peloponnese as well as on what was imported into it belonged to those who held the keys. And to later times this remained ever so.

But to the Corinthians of later times still greater advantages were added, for also the Isthmian games, which were celebrated there, were wont to draw crowds of people.

The adjective 'wealthy' is taken from Homer in a passage cited by Strabo some pages earlier (8:6.19). In listing the troops commanded by Agamemnon in the war against Troy the poet mentions those who came from 'wealthy Corinth' (*Iliad*, 2:570), but it is not clear whether he was referring to the city or the region.

The sources of that wealth were, firstly, the revenues generated by the passage of goods across the Isthmus, both from sea to sea and in and out of the Peloponnese, and secondly, the money spent by the vast crowds who came for the Isthmian games (cf. Pausanias, p. 14 above). The city also had other sources of income (cf. 20c and 23d).

The Early History of Corinth

20b. The Bacchiadae, a rich and numerous and illustrious family, became tyrants of Corinth and held their empire for nearly 200 years, and without disturbance reaped the fruits of commerce. Cypselus overthrew these and himself became tyrant, and his house endured for three generations; and an evidence of the wealth of his house is the offering which Cypselus dedicated at Olympia, a huge statue of beaten gold. Again, Demaratus, one of the men who had been in power at Corinth, fleeing from the seditions there, carried with him so much wealth from his home to Tyrrhenia that not only he himself became the ruler of the city that admitted him, but his son was made king of the Romans.

The Bacchiadae have already been dealt with (p. 36 above). Cypselus came to power in 655 B.C. He expanded the trade in ceramics, and founded colonies in Leucas, Ambracia and Anactorium on the route to Italy. His son was Periander (c. 625-585 B.C.), constructer of the *diolkos* and the first to propose cutting a canal through the Isthmus. His concern to find employment for all his subjects resulted in a tremendous development in art, industry, and commerce. He was succeeded by his nephew Psammeticus, who was very quickly assassinated. These were the golden years of Corinth which established the pattern for its future.

The City of Love

20c. And the temple of Aphrodite was so rich that it owned more than a thousand temple-slaves, prostitutes, whom both men and women had dedicated to the goddess. And therefore it was also on account of these women that the city was crowded with people and grew rich. For instance, the ship-captains freely squandered their money, and hence the proverb, "Not for every man is the voyage to Corinth." Moreover, it is said that a certain prostitute said to the woman who reproached her with the charge that she did not like to work or touch wool, "Yet such as I am, in this short time I have taken down three webs."

Another source of Corinth's wealth was the crowds attracted by the delights offered by the 1000-plus sacred prostitutes who served the temple of Aphrodite. Many New Testament introductions and commentaries have stressed this aspect because it appears to provide an explanation for the attention that Paul was obliged to give to sexual problems in 1 Cor 5-7. However, the context clearly indicates that Strabo is here referring to the pre-146 B.C. city and not to the newly constituted Roman colony that he visited in 29 B.C. Then he saw only a 'small temple of Aphrodite' (21b); the same adjective would apply to the two that Pausanias mentions (pp. 28 and 39 above). The excavations have not revealed any temple of Aphrodite of any period capable of accommodating the numbers mentioned here.

Even for the pre-146 B.C. city the reliability of Strabo's account has been called into question (Conzelmann, 1967). Were Strabo correct, Corinth would be unique among the cities of Greece. Sacred prostitution was never a Greek custom and, were Corinth an exception, the silence of all other ancient authors becomes impossible to explain. What appears to have happened is that Strabo combined elements from a number of different sources to produce a totally distorted picture. He knew of women servants in the temple of Aphrodite (but they were not prostitutes); he was aware of Corinth's reputation for licentiousness (see below); and he may have misunderstood an ode of Pindar (cf. Athenaeus, p. 132 below). All this he put together in the light of his own experience of Comana in Pontus where there was "a multitude of women who make gain from their persons, most of whom are dedicated to the goddess, for in a way the city is a lesser Corinth" (*Geography*, 12:3.36). Sacred prostitution was common in the east, and what Strabo in fact did was to make Corinth a 'greater Comana', on the false assumption that the same sort of thing must have happened there.

Corinth had a certain reputation in sexual matters. Aristophanes (c. 450-385 B.C.) coined the verb *korinthiazesthai* 'to act like a Corinthian', i.e. to practice fornication. Plays with the title *Korinthiastes* 'The Whoremonger' were written by Philetaerus (4th cent. B.C.) and Poliochus (Athenaeus, *Deipnosophistae*, 313c, 559a). In his list of the special products of each Greek city Antiphanes (c. 388-311 B.C.) associates 'bed-spreads' with Corinth (Athenaeus, *Deip.*, 27d). Plato (c. 429-347 B.C.) used *korinthia koré* 'a Corinthian girl' to mean a prostitute (*Republic*, 404D).

It is doubtful that the situation at Corinth was any worse than in other port-cities of the eastern Mediterranean. It seems likely that its reputation was the result of assiduous Athenian propaganda (Conzelmann, 1975: 12). The fruits of commerce are often envied by those dedicated to culture. Plutarch says, "We laugh at the stupidity of the man who asserts that there is a better moon at Athens than at Corinth." (*Moralia,* 601C); he might have, but there were many who didn't (cf. Favorinus, p. 100 below).

The proverb 'Not for every man is the voyage to Corinth' was known in Rome. About 20 B.C. it was quoted by Horace (*Letters*, 1:17.36) in a political context where the meaning is 'Only the tough survive'. This may well have been the original connotation; business was at least as cutthroat at Corinth as anywhere else. However, 'Watch your trousers' is certainly the meaning it has in Strabo, particularly because of the pun in the prostitute's response. As the note in the Loeb edition points out, 'to take down three webs' can also mean 'to lower three masts', i.e. to satisfy three seamen.

The Description of Corinth

21a. The situation of the city, as described by Hieronymus and Eudoxus and others, and from what I myself saw after the recent restoration of the city by the Romans, is about as follows:

A lofty mountain with a perpendicular height of 3î stadia, and an ascent of as much as 30 stadia, ends in a sharp peak. It is called Acrocorinth, and its northern side is the steepest.

Beneath it lies the city in a level, trapezium-shaped place close to the very base of Acrocorinth. Now the circuit of the city itself used to be as much as 40 stadia, and all of it that was unprotected by the mountain was enclosed by a wall. Even the mountain itself, Acrocorinth, used to be comprehended within the circuit of this wall wherever wall-building was possible. And when I went up the mountain the ruins of the encircling wall were plainly visible; the whole perimeter amounted to about 85 stadia. On its other sides the mountain is less steep, though here too it rises to a considerable height and is conspicuous all round.

Strabo's description of the restored city is based partly on descriptions left by Hieronymus of Rhodes (c. 290-230 B.C.) and Eudoxus of Cnidus (c. 408-355 B.C.) and partly on what he himself experienced. The figures presumably derive from his sources, but it is doubtful if anything else does. All that he mentions could be seen from the route he professes to follow. In fact, he gives little beyond a general outline whose details need to be filled in from Pausanias (cf. p. 23 above).

Acrocorinth is 575 meters high, and served as the citadel of Corinth from at least the 4th cent. B.C. It anchored the 10 km perimeter wall which enclosed an area of about 4 Sq. kms (cf. fig. 4). When Strabo saw it in 29 B.C. this wall was in the ruined state in which Mummius had left it in 146 B.C. (cf. 23a). At this stage, however, the colony was only 15 years old and there were higher priorities than defense. The condition of the walls had deteriorated even further in Paul's day. Peace had been firmly established throughout the region for two centuries, and there was no incentive to invest the massive sums that rebuilding would require. On the contrary, the walls were exploited as a quarry of cut stone. Apparently only the gates were preserved as a symbolic statement of the extent of the city, the greatest in all Greece. Both Pausanias (p. 22 above) and Dio Chrysostom (p. 96 below) reveal that even in the second century A.D. the built-up area had not reached the line of the walls.

The Summit of Acrocorinth

21b. The summit has a small temple of Aphrodite, and below the summit is the spring Peirene, which, although it has no overflow, is always full of transparent, potable water.

They say that the spring at the base of the mountain is the joint result of pressure from this and other subterranean veins of water — a spring which flows out into the city in such quantity that it affords a fairly large supply of water.

There is a good supply of wells throughout the city, as also, they say, on Acrocorinth, but I myself did not see the latter wells. At any rate when Euripides says, "I am come, having left Acrocorinth that is washed on all sides, the sacred hill-city of Aphrodite," one should take 'washed on all sides' as meaning in the depths of the mountain, since wells and subterranean pools extend through it. Alternatively one could assume that in early times Peirene used to rise over the surface and flow down the sides of the mountain.

Here, they say, Pegasus, a winged horse which sprang from the neck of the Gorgon Medusa when her head was cut off, was caught while drinking by Bellerophon. And the same horse, it is said, caused Hippu-crene to spring up on Helicon when he struck with his hoof the rock that is below that mountain.

And at the foot of Peirene is the Sisypheium, which preserves no inconsiderable ruins of a temple, or royal palace, made of white marble.

In addition to the small temple of Aphrodite which Strabo saw there was also a tiny temple of Venus on the west side of the agora (cf. Pausanias, p. 28 above).

The description of Corinth as "the sacred hill-city of Aphrodite" in the citation from Euripides (c. 485-406 B.C.)

reflects the reputation of the city discussed above (20c). The original meaning of the quotation was that Corinth was 'washed on both sides', i.e. by the Corinthian and Saronic Gulfs (cf. fig. 1); compare Horace's phrase "double-sea Corinth" (*Odes*, 1:7.2). Strabo's misinterpretation derived from the speculation of his sources that there was a connection between the two springs, Upper Peirene on Acrocorinth and Lower Peirene just off the agora (n. 24 in fig. 5); obviously this was no more than an effort to explain the identity of name.

For the association of Sisyphus with Corinth, see Pausanias (p. 8 above). Bellerophon, the brave and beautiful, was his grandson. Both were legendary kings of Corinth (cf. Pausanias, pp. 33 and 35 above). Helicon is the largest mountain in Boeotia. The same legend is told of Corinth by Dio Chrysostom (*Discourses*, 36:46), and Pausanias mentions a fountain whose water flowed through the foot of Pegasus (p. 30 above).

These are the only mythological associations of Corinth that Strabo mentions, and are in continuity with those reported by Pausanias. Thus, for the 1st cent. A.D. we can assume that at least the myths of Aphrodite, Sisyphus, and Bellerophon and Pegasus exercised a certain influence on the minds of the inhabitants.

The View From Acrocorinth

20c. From the summit, looking towards the north, one can see Parnassus and Helicon — lofty snow-clad mountains — and the Crisaean Gulf, which lies at the foot of the two mountains and is surrounded by Phocis, Boeotia, and Megaris, and by the parts of Corinthia and Sicyonia which lie across the gulf opposite to Phocis, that is, towards the west.

And above all these countries lie the Oneian Mountains, as they are called, which extend as far as Boeotia and Cithaeron from the Sceironian Rocks, that is, from the road that leads along these rocks towards Attica.

In the first paragraph Strabo describes what can be seen looking towards the north and the west, i.e. the two sides of the Corinthian Gulf, but his account is too condensed to be fully accurate. Megaris, for example, is far to the east of the Crisaean Gulf, the indentation with modern Itea at its head.

In the second paragraph he is looking to the east along the Isthmus (cf. fig. 1), and he confuses the Oneian Mountains, which are actually south-east of Corinth, with the Gerania Mountains, which constituted the limits of Corinthian territory on that side.

Strabo does not mention the view to the south, because he had done so previously:

> Cleonae is a town situated by the road that leads from Argos to Corinth, on a hill which is surrounded by dwellings on all sides and is well fortified.... And here too, between Cleonae and Phlius, are Nemea and the sacred precinct in which the Argives are wont to celebrate the Nemean games, and the scene of the myth of the Nemean lion, and the village of Bembina. Cleonae is 120 stadia from Argos, and 80 from Corinth. I myself have beheld the settlement from Acrocorinth. (8:6.19).

These towns are located in fig. 1. The killing of the Nemean lion was one of the labours of Heracles. It is this passage which guarantees that Strabo actually went to the top of Acrocorinth.

The Harbours of Corinth

> 22a. The beginning of the seaboard on the two sides is, on the one side, Lechaeum, and on the other, Cenchreae, a village and a harbour distant about 70 stadia from Corinth. Now this latter they use for the trade from Asia, but Lechaeum for that from Italy. Lechaeum lies beneath the city, and does not contain many residences, but long walls about 12 stadia in length have been built on both sides of the road that leads to Lechaeum.

The two harbours are located in fig. 1, and what is known about them has been dealt with above (p. 18). At this period the lack of houses at Lechaeum is not surprising because the new colonists would have tended to huddle together. As regards the long walls (cf. fig. 4), Strabo should not be understood to mean that these had been restored, whereas the other walls (21a) were not.

Description of the Isthmus

22b. The shore that extends from here to Pagae in Megaris is washed by the Corinthian Gulf. It is concave, and with the shore on the other side, at Schoenus, which is near Cenchreae, it forms the Diolcus.

In the interval between Lechaeum and Pagae there used to be in early times the oracle of the Acraean Hera; and here too is Olmiae, the promontory that forms the gulf in which are situated Oenoe and Pagae, the latter a stronghold of the Megarians, as the former is of the Corinthians.

From Cenchreae one comes to Schoenus, where is the narrow part of the Isthmus, I mean the Diolcus. Then one comes to Crommyonia. Off this shore lie the Saronic and Eleusinian Gulfs, which in a way are the same, and border on the Hermonic Gulf.

On the Isthmus is also the temple of the Isthmian Poseidon, in the shade of a grove of pine-trees, where the Corinthians used to celebrate the Isthmian games.

Crommyon is a village in Corinthia, though in earlier times it was in Megaris, and in it is laid the scene of the myth of the Crommyonian sow, which, it is said, was the mother of the Caledonian boar; and, according to tradition, the destruction of this sow was one of the labours of Theseus.

The places mentioned in this section are located in fig. 1, for Strabo is here dealing with the two coasts of Corinth as they extend to the north-east.

The Diolcus was a paved road joining the Corinthian and Saronic Gulfs. Letter-forms on some of the paving stones are of the 6th cent. B.C. and suggest that it was first constructed by Periander (see 20b). Excavations have revealed a dock and 460 meters of road on the west side of the Isthmus. The width varies from 3.4 to 6 meters, but the channels cut in the pavement to guide the wheels of the movable wooden platform (the *holkos*) are only 1.5 meters apart. Here we have unambiguous evidence that only rather small craft could be transported across the Isthmus. The width of the road further indicates that no provision was made for passing. Hence, there must have been some system of signals to ensure that there were not simultaneous starts from both sides. The last recorded use of the Diolcus was in the 9th cent. A.D. For all details see Wiseman, 1978:45-46.

The sanctuary of Poseidon and the Isthmian games are dealt with on pp. 10-17 above. The formulation of Strabo, particularly when contrasted with that used apropos of the Nemean games (p. 62 above), clearly indicates that the games were not celebrated there when he passed in 29 B.C.

The City of Tenea

22c. Tenea is also in Corinthia, and in it is a temple of the Teneatan Apollo, and it is said that most of the colonists who accompanied Archias, the leader of the colonists to Syracuse, set out from there, and that afterwards Tenea prospered more than the other settlements, and finally even had a government of its own, and, revolting from the Corinthians, joined the Romans, and endured after the destruction of Corinth.

Mention is made of an oracle which was given to a certain man from Asia, who enquired whether it was better to change his home to Corinth: "Blest is Corinth, but Tenea for me!"

And it is said that Polybius reared Oedipus here. And it seems also that there is a kinship between the peoples of Tenedos and Tenea, through Tennes the son of Cycnus, as Aristotle says; and the similarity in the worship of Apollo among the two peoples affords strong indications of such kinship.

Apparently the reason why Strabo includes this information at just this point is that his survey of the southern Corinthia was controlled by the places mentioned in Homer's Catalogue of Ships (*Iliad*, 2:569ff.). Though located almost due south of Corinth (cf. fig. 1), Tenea did not appear in this list. Yet it merited inclusion here because it gave its name to one of the gates of Corinth (cf. fig. 4). We know this from Pausanias who, moreover, explains Homer's silence. Tenea was settled only after the Trojan war, and by Trojan prisoners taken at Tenedos (p. 41 above).

The Fall of Corinth

23a. The Corinthians, when they were subject to Philip, not only sided with him in his quarrel with the Romans, but individually behaved so contemptuously towards the Romans that certain persons ventured to pour down filth upon the Roman ambassadors when passing by their house.

For this and other offences, however, they soon paid the penalty, for a considerable army was sent thither, and the city itself was rased to the ground by Leucius Mummius. And the other countries as far as Macedonia became subject to the Romans, different commanders being sent into different countries, but the Sicyonians obtained most of the Corinthian territory.

The Romanophile side of Strabo's character comes strongly to the fore here; he evidently feels that the Corinthians had brought disaster upon themselves by their attitude towards the Romans. The Philip mentioned is Philip V of Macedon (238-179 B.C.), the Corinthians having traded their city to the Macedonians in 224 B.C. in return for aid against Sparta. Weakened by the Hannibalic War, Rome was forced to concede Philip's conquests in Illyria (205 B.C.) but, once recovered, it eased Philip out of the Peloponnese.

Control passed to the Achaean League, of which Corinth was a member, in 194 B.C. When the League proved more independent than anticipated, Rome decided to weaken it. In 147 B.C. a Roman delegation came to Corinth to announce Rome's desire that the League should be dissolved (Wiseman, 1979:459-461). It was perhaps in the pandemonium which followed this arrogant gesture that the episode reported by Strabo took place. War with Rome became inevitable the following year, when the League opened hostilities with Sparta. Corinth had few defenders when Mummius arrived at its gates in 146 B.C. because three armies of the League had been defeated by another Roman general in battles north of the Isthmus.

The Sack of Corinth

23b. Polybius, who speaks in a tone of pity of the events connected with the capture of Corinth, goes on to speak of the disregard shown by the army for the works of art and votive offerings; for he says that he was present and saw paintings that had been flung to the ground and saw the soldiers playing dice on them.

Among the paintings he names that of Dionysus by Aristeides, to which, according to some writers, the saying "Nothing in comparison with Dionysus" referred; and also the painting of Heracles in torture in the robe of Deianeira. Now I have not seen the latter, but I saw the Dionysus, a most beautiful work, on the walls of the temple of Ceres in Rome; but when recently the temple was burned, the painting disappeared with it.

And I may almost say that the most and best of the other dedicatory offerings at Rome came from there, and the cities in the neighbourhood of Rome also obtained some. For Mummius, being magnanimous rather than fond of art, as they say, readily shared with those who asked. When Leucullus built the temple of Good Fortune and a portico, he asked Mummius for the use of the statues which he had, saying that he would adorn the temple with them until the dedication and then give them back. However, he did not give them back, but dedicated them to the goddess, and then bade Mummius to take them away if he wished. But Mummius took it lightly, for he cared nothing about them, so that he gained more repute than the man who dedicated them.

For the description of the devastation Strabo uses an eye-witness, the Greek historian of Rome, Polybius (c. 203-120 B.C.); unfortunately, this part of his 40-book *Universal History* has been lost. The picture Strabo saw must have been that of Dionysus by Aristeides of Thebes who was active c. 360 B.C.; it could only have been on his first visit to Rome in 44 B.C. because the temple of Ceres was burnt in 31 B.C.

Nothing is said regarding the fate of the inhabitants, but this data is supplied by Pausanias (p. 42 above) and Dio Cassius (p. 128 below).

The Refounding of Corinth

23c. Now after Corinth had remained deserted for a long time, it was restored again, because of its favourable position, by the deified Caesar, who colonised it with people who for the most part belonged to the freedman class.

When these were removing the ruins and at the same time digging open the graves, they found numbers of terra-cotta reliefs, and also many bronze vessels. And since they admired the workmanship they left no grave unransacked. So that, well supplied with such things and disposing of them at a high price, they filled Rome with Corinthian "mortuaries," for thus they called the things taken from the graves, and in particular the earthenware.

Now at the outset the earthenware was very highly prized, like the bronzes of Corinthian workmanship, but later they ceased to care much for them, since the supply of earthen vessels failed and most of them were not even well executed.

By 44 B.C. the Romans had been in peaceful control of Greece for just a century, despite rather radical interventions in its political and economic structures (Larsen: 306-325). Thus, the choice of Corinth as the site of a colony is unlikely to have been dictated by military reasons. Indeed, the whole tone of Strabo's presentation would argue that 'the favourable position' was conceived in economic terms. This harmonises perfectly with the assertion that the majority of the new colonists were freedmen. There may have been some veterans, but in opposition to what Plutarch says (p. 107 below), they would have been a small minority.

Freedmen were slaves who had been freed, but who did not have the status of freemen. Under Roman law certain positions in the army and the public service were not open to them, and their former owners could claim certain services in return for the generosity shown in freeing them. The change in status made little difference to the life-style of most freedmen. The majority were the small shopkeepers, artisans, teachers, and secretaries; a group well categorized by the term 'poor' which Appian uses (p. 117 below). These were recruited because they formed the technical core without which no city can survive.

Other freedmen must have been men of initiative and vision who, through the training gained in the service of their former masters, were aware of the ways to acquire capital and to deploy it wisely. Some would surely have acted as the agents of investors in Rome who recognized the tremendous economic potential of the site of Corinth.

For both groups of freedmen the move to a new colony would have meant a step up the social ladder; the restrictions under which they legally laboured would have been rendered purely theoretical by distance. In addition, their children would have been full and free citizens in a land of golden opportunity.

The first colonists would also have numbered slaves and, of course, freemen willing to gamble on the advantages of being in on the ground-floor of an enterprise which promised great rewards. Once the new colony grew it would have attracted far-sighted entrepreneurs both from Greece and from the major trading countries in the eastern Mediterranean, notably Egypt. Such infusions of new capital in a prime commercial situation inevitably generated more wealth, and within 50 years of its foundation many of the citizens had become men of very considerable means; L. Castricius Regulus (cf. p. 14 above) is a case in point.

In order to gain capital, however, many of the first settlers turned to grave robbing. There was a ready market in Rome for Corinthian artifacts in terra-cotta and bronze, and the graves had not been looted by the army of Mummius. Interest in terra-cotta soon waned, but the desire for bronze waxed (cf. Propertius, p. 75 below). Well into the 1st cent. A.D. the avidity with which collectors sought Corinthian bronze could be termed a 'mania' by Pliny the Elder (p. 85 below). This latter implies that not all that passed for Corinthian bronze was a genuine antiquity, so it appears probable that certain of the new settlers found it profitable to restart the bronze industry. The bronze smithy discovered near the Lechaeum road (cf. Pausanias, p. 31 above) is dated to the first years of the colony, and two other installations, one on the west side of the forum and the other near the temple of Asclepius (cf. figs. 4 and 5), are dated to the 1st cent. A.D. (Wiseman, 1979:512).

Concluding Summary

23d. The city of Corinth, then, was always great and wealthy, and it was well equipped with men skilled both in the affairs of state and in the craftsman's arts; for both here and in Sicyon the arts of painting and modelling and all such arts of the craftsman flourished most.

The city had territory, however, that was not very fertile, but rifted and rough; and from this fact all have called Corinth "beetling," and use the proverb, "Corinth is both beetle-browed and full of hollows."

Having already dealt with the other sources of Corinth's wealth (cf. 20a and 20c), Strabo here underlines the city's productivity. The reference can only be to the pre-146 B.C. city. But on the basis of what has just been said regarding bronze-working, we can reasonably suppose that most of the traditional crafts were again developed in the Roman colony. Corinth had a name for quality products and it would be very strange if its energetic colonists had ignored the opportunity for gain that a good trading reputation implies (Wiseman, 1978:13).

The terrain around the city and towards the Isthmus is well described by the proverb quoted by Strabo. The soil is thin and erosion damage very noticeable; jagged edges of limestone project above the worn surface of the soft marl (Wiseman, 1978:9). The very fertile land evoked by Cicero (p. 46 above) lay to the west of Corinth in the coastal plain cut by the Nemean River (cf. fig. 1). "'How may I get rich, Son of Zeus and Leto?' The god mockingly replied: 'By acquiring what lies between Corinth and Sicyon,'" (Athenaeus, *Deipnosophistae*, 219a). The land was so valuable that the god's response is the equivalent to our telling a contemporary to buy the island of Manhattan.

GEOGRAPHY, 10:5.4

> Although Delos had become so famous, yet the rasing of Corinth to the ground by the Romans increased its fame still more; for the importers changed their business to Delos because they were attracted both by the immunity which the temple enjoyed and by the convenient situation of the harbour; for it is happily situated for those who are sailing from Italy and Greece to Asia.
>
> The general festival is a kind of commercial affair, and it was frequented by Romans more than by any other people, even when Corinth was still in existence.
>
> When the Athenians took the island they at the same time took good care of the importers as well as of the religious rites. But when the generals of Mithridates, and the tyrant who caused it to revolt, visited Delos, they completely ruined it, and when the Romans again got the island, after the king withdrew to his homeland, it was desolate; and it has remained in an impoverished condition until the present time. It is now held by the Athenians.

In order to destroy the trade of Rhodes the Romans made the tiny island of Delos (5.6 x 1.2 kms), the center of the Cyclades, a free port (166 B.C.). It was this, in addition to its location, which attracted the merchants who had used Corinth until its destruction in 146 B.C. The next fifty or sixty years were the acme of commercial Delos. The volume of business is graphically illustrated by Strabo, "Delos could both admit and send away 10,000 slaves in a single day; whence arose the proverb, 'Merchant, sail in, unload your ship, everything has been sold.'" (14:5.2), and amply documented in the temple records (Larsen: 334-357); only by extrapolation from this source can we form any idea of the volume of the east-west trade of Corinth.

The decline of Delos set in when it was devastated by Mithridates, king of Pontus, in 88 B.C. Rebuilt with Roman aid the following year, it was sacked by pirates in 69 B.C. Despite its advantages the isolated island was too vulnerable, and it would have been surprising had not the idea of restoring Corinth entered the minds of certain Roman officials. However, it took Julius Caesar to act.

GEOGRAPHY, 17:3.25

But the Provinces have been divided in different ways at different times, though at the present time they are as Augustus Caesar arranged them; for when his native land committed to him the foremost place of authority and he became established as lord for life of war and peace, he divided the whole of his empire into two parts, and assigned one portion to himself and the other to the Roman people; to himself, all parts that had need of a military guard (that is, the part that was barbarian and in the neighbourhood of tribes not yet subdued, or lands that were sterile and difficult to bring under cultivation, so that, being unprovided with everything else, but well provided with strongholds, they would try to throw off the bridle and refuse obedience), and to the Roman people all the rest, in so far as it was peaceable and easy to rule without arms.

He divided each of the two portions into several Provinces, of which some are called "Provinces of Caesar" and the others "Provinces of the People." And to the "Provinces of Caesar" Caesar sends legati and procurators, dividing the countries in different ways at different times and administering them as the occasion requires, whereas to the "Provinces of the People" the people send praetors or proconsuls, and these Provinces also are brought under different divisions whenever expediency requires.

But at the outset Caesar organised the Provinces of the People by creating, first, two consular provinces; I mean (1) Libya, in so far as it was subject to the Romans, except the part which was formerly subject to Juba and is now subject to Ptolemy his son, and (2) the part of Asia that lies this side the Halys River and the Taurus, except the countries of the Galatians and of the tribes which had been subject to Amyntas, and also of Bithynia and the Propontis; and, secondly, ten praetorial provinces, first, in Europe and the islands near it, I mean (1) Iberia Ulterior, as it is called, in the neighbourhood of the Baetis and Anas Rivers, (2) Narbonitis in Celtica, (3) Sardo together with Cyrnus, (4) Sicily, (5 and 6) Macedonia and, in Illyria, the country next to Epeirus, (7) Achaea as far as Thessaly and Aetolia and Acarnania and certain Epeirotic tribes which border on Macedonia, (8) Crete along with Cyrenaea, (9) Cypros, and (10) Bithynia along with the Propontis and certain parts of the Pontus.

But the rest of the Provinces are held by Caesar; and to some of these he sends as curators men of consular rank, to others men of praetorian rank, and to others men of the rank of knights. Kings, also, and potentates and decarchies are now, and always have been, in Caesar's portion.

This text is the earliest attestation of Augustus' creation of two types of Roman province in 27 B.C.; they are now more commonly known as Imperial and Senatorial provinces. Achaia, to which Corinth belonged, is listed as a Senatorial province and was, in consequence, governed by a proconsul. However, in A.D. 15, "since Achaia and Macedonia protested against the heavy taxation, it was decided to relieve them of their proconsular government for the time being and transfer them to the emperor." (Tacitus, *Annals*, 1:76). What this meant in practice is that they were added to the Imperial province of Moesia (*Annals*, 1:80). Since it is difficult to believe that Corinth was short of money, the true cause must have been inefficient administration. This was an endemic problem in Senatorial provinces whose goverors remained in office for only one year. Imperial officials, on the contrary, served at the pleasure of the emperor and normally retained their posts for considerable periods. Achaia was returned to the Senate in A.D. 44 (see Suetonius, p. 115 below).

The impression given by Strabo is of two virtually independent administrative systems, and this may have been the intention of Augustus. However, the reality of the distinction must be tested against what actually happened in practice, and this is admirably summarised by F. Millar, "When the evidence is assembled, the notion of two separate administrative hierarchies, whose lines of demarcation were crossed only by the Emperor in occasional 'interventions', becomes entirely untenable. The Emperor did not govern the Imperial provinces either as a whole or individually 'through' his *legati* [legates]; like proconsuls, the *legati* governed their provinces themselves. In no sense whatsoever did the Senate 'control' the senatorial provinces, and the proconsuls were not 'responsible' to it. Both the Emperor and the Senate, predominantly of course the former, made regulations (sometimes jointly) affecting all the provinces. The Emperor could deal directly with provinces of both types or with communities within them. The Senate is not attested as dealing with any Imperial province as a whole, but is found dealing with individual places in these provinces. The sole concrete distinctions are in the direct relations between the Emperor and *legati* and proconsuls. *Legati* received Imperial *mandata* [instructions] from the beginning, proconsuls (probably) from the first half of the second century. The Emperor, invariably it seems when stimulated by some other source of information, pressure or complaint from within the province, might initiate correspondence with either type of governor. But *legati* are attested initiating such correspondence quite commonly in the first century — to make reports or to ask advice — while proconsuls began to do so under Hadrian." (1966:165)

Since the last lines of this citation are directly relevant to the question of the proconsul Gallio's report to the emperor Claudius (see below p. 141), it is important to note that under certain circumstances the Senate surrendered to the Emperor its right to appoint proconsuls. Since these were nominated by the latter and not chosen by lot, they were known as *proconsules extra sortem* 'proconsuls outside the lottery system.' To the extent that they were assimilated to *legati* they presumably exercised the same initiative in correspondence with the Emperor.

LIVY

Titius Livius was born in Padua in 59 B.C. As he was encouraged by Augustus in his historical studies, so he in turn encouraged Claudius. He worked on his *History of Rome* for forty years. All but thirty-five of the original 142 books have been lost, including those in which he must have spoken of the fall of Corinth and its resurrection under Julius Caesar. He died in A.D. 17.

HISTORY OF ROME, 45:28

>After offering sacrifice at Athens to Minerva, the presiding deity of the Acropolis, Paulus left for Corinth, which he reached on the second day. This city was at that time,

> before its destruction, a place of outstanding beauty; its citadel, within the walls, rising up to an immense height, abounding in springs of water, while the Isthmus separates by this narrow passage two neighbouring seas to the east and to the west. From there Paulus visited Scyon and Argos, two famous cities, and went on to Epidaurus, a city no match for those others in wealth, but renowned for the famous temple of Ascelpius.

Paulus is Aemilius Paulus commander-in-chief of the Roman forces in Greece and his tour of historic sites is dated to the late summer of 167 B.C. Evidently tourism also contributed to the prosperity of Corinth. The time taken for the journey from Athens to Corinth is confirmed by Dio Chrysostom (p. 95 below). The citadel, of course, is Acrocorinth.

PROPERTIUS

Born between 54 and 43 B.C. in Assisi, Sextus Propertius came to Rome when his family was impoverished by the redistribution of land in 41 B.C. There, around 29-24 B.C., he became enamoured of a lady named Cynthia whose affections were not as fixed as his were. This turbulent relationship inspired most of his four books of *Elegies*. The latest date that can be assigned to any poem of Propertius is 16 B.C.; he died sometime in the following fourteen years.

ELEGIES, 3:5.3-6

> My heart is not a victim of the love of gold; I hate it.
> My thirst is not quenched at the lip of a precious stone.
> I don't have a thousand pairs of oxen ploughing the rich Campania. I am poor and don't profit from your ruin, O Corinth, by possessing your bronzes.

To put Corinthian bronze in the same category as gold, precious stones, and vast estates, gives a very precise idea of its value, and explains the market-demand, implied by Strabo (p. 67 above), which existed in Rome in the last decades of the 1st cent. B.C. It was not to diminish in the century which followed (cf. Pliny the Elder, p. 88 below).

ELEGIES, 3:21.1-24

> So be it, I leave for wise Athens, the great and long voyage will diminish the pangs of love.... I have only a single remedy, Cynthia, to change countries; then you will be as far from my heart as from my eyes.
>
> So my friends, let us put the boat afloat, draw lots for the teams of oarsmen, and attach to the top of the mast a sail of good fortune. The wind is favourable, and the liquid road lies before the seamen. Farewell, you towers of Rome, and you too my friends. In spite of all I wave goodbye to even you my mistress. The Adriatic will take me; its waves will become familiar and I must implore the favour of its gods.
>
> Having traversed the Ionian Sea, the tired vessel will furl its sails in the calm waters of Lechaeum, and I shall continue on foot. In haste, despite my fatigue, I shall cross the Isthmus which separates the two seas. Once in Piraeus I shall go up by the route of Theseus between the arms of the Long Walls.

In order to still the pain of unrequited love, Propertius proposes to leave Rome and bury himself in Athens. He had never been out of Italy, so the route he describes must have been the easiest and most natural one between the two cities (cf. Philo, p. 83 below). Mention of the Adriatic Sea supposes a departure point on the east coast of Italy. Lechaeum was the western port of Corinth, and the unhappy lover would have had to walk to the eastern port of Cenchreae (cf. p. 17 above) to take ship again for Piraeus the harbour of Athens. The reverse route is described by Philostratus (p. 131 below). Its situation on the Isthmus meant that Corinth had many visitors whose real concerns were elsewhere; even if they passed some of their money certainly remained.

The mention of the route of Theseus highlights the second-hand nature of Propertius' information, because this was the land route from Corinth to Athens, which is described by Dio Chrysostom (p. 96 below), and which was travelled in the reverse direction by Pausanias (p. 19 above).

VITRUVIUS

No dates can be assigned to the life of Vitruvius Pollio. We know only that he had known Julius Caesar and that he served as a military engineer under Augustus. It was to the latter that he dedicated his work *On Architecture* which must have been published prior to 27 B.C. It is a synthesis of his own practical experience and the discoveries of his predecessors in engineering and architecture, and remained an influential manual for almost 500 years.

ON ARCHITECTURE, 5:5.1,7-8

1. Hence in accordance with these enquiries, bronze vases are to be made in mathematical ratios corresponding with the size of the theatre. They are to be so made that, when they are touched, they can make a sound from one to another of a fourth, a fifth and so on to the second octave.

Then compartments are made among the seats of the theatre, and the vases are to be so placed that they do not touch the wall, and have an empty space around them and above. They are to be placed upside down. On the side looking towards the stage, they are to have wedges put under them not less than half a foot high. Against these cavities openings are to be left in the faces of the lower steps two feet long and half a foot high. . . .

7. Someone will say, perhaps, that many theatres are built

every year in Rome without taking any account of these matters. He will be mistaken in this.

All public wooden theatres have several wooden floors which naturally resound. We can observe this also from those who sing to the zither, who when they wish to sing with a louder tone, turn to the wooden scenery, and, with this help, gain resonance for their voice. But when theatres are built of solids, that is of rubble walling, stone or marble which cannot resound, the use of bronze vases is to be followed.

8. But if you ask in what theatre this is done, we cannot show any at Rome, but we must turn to the regions of Italy, and to many Greek cities. We find a precedent in Lucius Mummius who destroyed the theatre at Corinth, and transported these bronze vessels to Rome, and dedicated them, from the spoils, at the temple of Luna.

Further, many clever architects, who in towns of moderate size have built theatres, have chosen, for cheapness' sake, earthenware vessels with similar sounds, and arranging them in this way have produced very useful effects.

W. Harris was the first to point out that this use of Corinthian bronze furnished an illustration of the 'sounding brass' mentioned by Paul in 1 Cor 13:1. Vases placed upside down, and tilted by wedges which permitted them to be tuned, contributed only a resonant hum which gave body to the speaker's voice; their sound in itself was unintelligible. The theatre at Corinth had been restored by Paul's time (Wiseman, 1979:521), but none of the reports or drawings indicate any provision for such resonance enhancers. It is not impossible that Paul saw them elsewhere in the East.

One may legitimately wonder how Vitruvius knew the purpose of the vases that Mummius brought back from Corinth in 146 B.C., and the question of whether he was correct is raised by his own admission that none of the stone theatres at Rome had resonance enhancers. In fact, at the time he wrote there appears to have been only one, the 27,000 place theatre of Pompey which was dedicated in 55

B.C. The two others were later; the 7,700 place theatre of Balbus was laid out in 13 B.C. and the 14,000 place theatre of Marcellus was completed in 11 B.C. (Carcopino: 244). It is very difficult to see how such sound aids could have been effective under these conditions; the background noise of such numbers of people would have set up vibrations that could not but interfere with the fine tuning that the resonance enhancers demanded. The situation in the theatre at Corinth, which could hold 14,000, would have been no different, particularly when one remembers that the spectators would not have been the well-disciplined theatre-goers to whom we are accustomed. Thus, as regards very large theatres, Vitruvius' approach appears to be highly theoretical. It might have worked in much smaller buildings, and it is a pity that he does not mention by name any of the provincial cities in which he claims the phenomenon existed. Theatres at Caesarea Maritima and Scythopolis in Palestine and Aezani in Phrygia are thought to contain the appropriate niches (Plommer).

PHILO

Born c. 30 B.C. in Alexandria, he spent all his life in his native city. The greater part of his career was devoted to an exposition of the Pentateuch in terms designed to make it both comprehensible and palatable to those brought up on Greek philosophy. Eventually, he became head of the Jewish community in Alexandria, and had to deal with the very difficult situation that developed when the Roman governor of Egypt, Aulus Avillius Flaccus (A.D. 32-38), did not repress violently anti-semitic demonstrations.

Not long after the trial, exile, and execution of Flaccus in A.D. 38, Philo wrote *In Flaccum*, a masterpiece of vindictive gloating, to prove that God protects the Jews. In A.D. 39-41 Philo headed the delegation of Alexandrian Jews to

Rome. No settlement had been reached when the emperor Gaius was murdered on 24 January 41, and it was probably during this period of waiting that Philo completed the *Legatio ad Gaium* (Smallwood, 1970:151). The great philosopher died in A.D. 45.

LEGATIO AD GAIUM, 281-282

> 281. As for the Holy City, I must say what befits me to say. While she, as I have said, is my native city she is also the mother city, not of one country Judaea, but of most of the others in virtue of the colonies sent out at divers times to the neighbouring lands Egypt, Phoenicia, and Syria (the so-called Coele Syria as well as Syria proper), to lands lying far away, Pamphylia, Cilicia, most of Asia up to Bithynia and the corners of Pontus, similarly also into Europe, Thessaly, Boeotia, Macedonia, Aetolia, Attica, Argos, Corinth, and most of the best parts of the Peloponnese.
> 282. And not only are the mainlands full of Jewish colonies but also the most esteemed of the islands Euboea, Cyprus, and Crete. I say nothing of the countries beyond the Euphrates, for except for a small part they all, Babylon and the other satrapies whose surrounding land is fertile, have Jewish inhabitants.

With the exception of the mention of Mesopotamia at the end, this list of the Jewish Diaspora (taken from a letter of Agrippa I, cf. n. 276) moves anti-clockwise around the eastern Mediterranean. The fact that most of the names in the catalogue are of geographical regions gives special prominence to the three cities. The special attention accorded to Babylon is only to be expected, for it had a large Jewish population since the Exile (586-538 B.C.), but it is a little surprising to find Argos and Corinth singled out, particularly since the Peloponnese as a region is also mentioned. Despite the complete silence of all other ancient sources, it would appear that we must conclude that they both had particularly large and vital Jewish communities.

The only evidence of Jewish presence so far revealed by the excavations has been a lintel inscribed with the words [*Syna*]*gôgê Hebr*[*aiôn*] 'Synagogue of the Hebrews' (photo in Wiseman, 1979: plate 5 n. 8). The lettering is very crude and the date cannot be fixed with any precision. On the analogy of the situation at Rome, where there was one Synagogue of the Hebrews (Barrett: 51) and at least four others named for notable benefactors (Smallwood, 1981:138), this lintel may belong to the oldest synagogue in Corinth.

In 142 B.C. a Jewish presence in Sicyon (cf. fig. 1) is attested by 1 Macc 15:23. It is not impossible that this community was constituted, or at least augmented, by Jewish refugees from Corinth when it was destroyed in 146 B.C., because Corinth had always been a much more important center of basically the same craft industries (cf. Strabo, p. 67-68 above). If this were in fact the case, Jews from Sicyon probably constituted the nucleus of the community in Roman Corinth. Its numbers would have been significantly augmented after A.D. 67 when, according to Josephus (*Jewish War*, 3:540), Vespasian sent 6000 young men to work on the canal of Nero. Most of these would have become freedmen eventually. Others came from Palestine during and after the revolt of A.D. 132-5. Tryphon presents himself to Justin as "a refugee from the recent war, and at present a resident of Greece, especially of Corinth" (*Dialogue with Tryphon,* 1).

Information on Greek Jewry is virtually non-existent, so as regards the community at Corinth we are forced to extrapolate from what is known elsewhere in the Diaspora.

The most comprehensive statement of Jewish legal rights in the Diaspora is the decree of Augustus dated A.D. 2/3 preserved by Josephus in *Antiquities* 16:162-5. They were permitted to follow their own customs. Hence, the right to assemble in synagogues, to send money to Jerusalem, to be exempt from any civic activity that would violate the sabbath or their consciences (Smallwood, 1981:120-143). In virtue of such legislation, applicable throughout the empire, the Jewish community at Corinth was perhaps first recognised as a *collegium*, because of the Roman character of the colony, but by the time of Paul it might have been considered a *politeuma*, as was common in the cities of the East. A *politeuma* was a corporation of aliens with permanent right of domicile and empowered to manage its internal affairs through its own officials (Smallwood, 1981:225). As such Jews enjoyed a civic existence, but were not citizens in the full sense and did not enjoy the privileges of this status. A number in consequence aspired to it, and their refusal to assume the concommitant financial burden of participation in imperial or civic cults led to outbursts of antisemitism (*Antiquities*, 12:126; Daniel).

In the 1st cent. A.D. synagogues appear to have been deliberately made inconspicuous. Each one was headed by an *archisynagogos* ('ruler of the synagogue' Acts 18:8,17), and inscriptions indicate that this and other important functions were fulfilled by women (Brooten, *Women Leaders in the Ancient Synagogue,* Chico:SP, 1982). Women were not segregated at worship.

There is little evidence to support the claim of Mt 23:15 that Jews were active proselytizers (Kraabel, 1982:451). According to Josephus, they maintained an open-door policy to sincere inquirers but did not encourage even casual contacts with the merely curious (*Contra Appion*, 2:209-10). Converts were attracted, particularly since circumcision was not always required (McEleney; Horsley: 41), but the statistics are not impressive (PW Supp. 9:1264). The existence of a numerous group called the 'God-fearers' is not confirmed; it is probably a literary creation of Luke in Acts (Kraabel, 1981). The historical reality may have been pagans whose searching brought them into loose contact with the synagogue but who could not bring themselves to commitment until their indecisiveness was ended by Paul's forceful preaching.

As regards the social and economic position of Jews in the Diaspora the evidence suggests that they were a microcosm of the empire as a whole. They are found in the whole range of occupations from the most prestigious to the most degrading. No branch of trade or commerce is unrepresented. Perhaps at Corinth the "ship-owner, merchant, and artisan" tended to be prominent as at Alexandria (*In Flaccum*, 57). Among Jews one finds the same proportion of rich to poor as in society generally. Details are given by S. Applebaum, in *The Jewish People in the First Century,* 2:701-27.

IN FLACCUM, 151-156

> 151. Flaccus was to be exiled to the most miserable of the Aegean islands, called Gyara, had he not found an intercessor in Lepidus who enabled him to exchange Gyara for Andros, the island which lies nearest to it. He then again travelled along the road to Brundisium....
> 154. Having passed through the Ionian Gulf he sailed upon the sea which extends to Corinth, a spectacle to the Peloponnesian cities on the sea-board when they heard of his sudden change of fortune. For whenever he disembarked the people flocked thither, the baser natures out of malice, the rest, whose way is to find lessons of wisdom in the fate of others, to sympathize.
> 155. And crossing the Isthmus from Lechaeum to the opposite coast and coming down to Cenchreae, the port of Corinth, he was forced by his guards, who refused him any kind of intermission to embark at once on a small merchant vessel and put to sea, where under the violence of a contrary wind he suffered a thousand discomforts and only with difficulty arrived storm-tossed at Piraeus.
> 156. When the tempest ceased he coasted along Attica to Cape Sunium and then continued his journey along the series of islands, namely Helene, Cia, Cynthus, and the rest, which lie in a row one after another, to that which was to be the end of his journey, the island of the Andrians.

It is as unlikely that Philo had any first-hand information on Flaccus' route to exile as that the cities on the south coast of the Corinthian Gulf would have been interested in the fate of a Roman administrator of Egypt. Nonetheless, Philo gives a very accurate picture of the normal route to the east via Corinth (cf. Propertius, p. 76 above), and in particular of the mode of operation of the small trading vessels of the period. As far as possible they stayed close to the coast, and made every effort to find a safe harbour for the night.

PETRONIUS

Little is certain about Petronius. His *praenomen* was either Titus or Gaius, and the dates of his birth and death are unknown. It is considered most probable that he is to be identified with the Petronius described by Tacitus (*Annales*, 16:17-19) as having been proconsul of Bithynia, and *consul suffectus* before assuming the post of Master of Pleasures at the corrupt court of Nero (A.D. 54-68). In A.D. 66 his rival Tigellinus poisoned the emperor's mind against him, and he was driven to commit suicide.

Petronius is remembered for his *Satiricon*, which is also known as the *Cena Trimalchionis*, a low novel of the loves and adventures of three dissolute young freedmen. Its style and language place it firmly around the middle of the 1st cent. A.D.

SATIRICON, 50

All the crowd applauded and cried with one voice, "Hail Gaius!" In his turn the cook was rewarded with a silver crown and a bumper served in a cup standing on a Corinthian plate. As Agamemnon examined the latter closely, Trimalcion said, "I am the only one to possess genuine Corinthian objects." I expected him to claim, with his usual conceit, that he had vases sent to him from Corinth, but he got out of it better than I had anticipated. "Do you want to know," he asked, "how I alone come to possess genuine Corinthian vases? It's very simple. I buy them from a fellow called Corinth! And what is Corinthian if not stuff that comes from Corinth! But don't for a moment imagine that I am stupid. I know perfectly well the origin of Corinthian bronzes. When he captured Illium, Hannibal, that shifty trickster, stacked all the statues of bronze, gold and silver on a pyre and set it alight. Their metals melted and combined to form an alloy which was then used to make plates, dishes, and figurines. That's how Corinthian bronze came to be. Made of all sorts of things fused into one, it's neither fish nor fowl. Excuse me for what I'm going to say but, for my part, I prefer glass. At least it does not smell."

Trimalcion's claim that Corinthian bronze was developed by accident harmonises with the legends in Plutarch (cf. p. 106 below), but no confidence can be accorded his erudition; whatever else he may have done Hannibal certainly did not sack Troy. However, the hint that Corinthian bronze had a peculiar odour is confirmed by Martial (c. A.D. 40-104) who says of Mamurra that "he took counsel of his nose whether the bronzes smelt of Corinth" (*Epigrams*, 9:59.11). Evidently connoisseurs believed that they could nose out the truth.

It is difficult to evaluate the scepticism implicit in the notion that the vases were not sent from Corinth. It could be an assumption that Trimalcion would not have undertaken the expense, but equally it could be rooted in an awareness that Corinthian bronze was no longer available. This ambiguity means that the text cannot be used to contradict Pausanias (cf. p. 29 above), particularly when he is supported by Plutarch (p. 104 below).

PLINY THE ELDER

Gaius Plinius Secundus is known as Pliny the Elder in order to distinguish him from his nephew, Gaius Plinius

Caecilius Secundus, called Pliny the Younger. Born in A.D. 23 he served as a cavalry officer in Germany in A.D. 47-57. Returning to Rome, he withdrew into prudent retirement when the emperor Nero started to run wild in A.D. 59. Towards the end of his reign he accepted an appointment as Procurator of Spain, but came back to Rome to become one of Vespasian's principal advisors when the latter became emperor in A.D. 69. He died 10 years later of asphyxiation at Castellammare when a scientific expedition to view at close quarters the eruption of Vesuvius which destroyed Pompeii turned into an heroic rescue operation during which he was trapped on the coast; a vivid picture of the episode is given by his nephew (*Letters*, 6:16).

Despite a busy official career he wrote 102 volumes and left 160 unpublished note-books. His nephew describes his work-habits (*Letters*, 3:5). Not a moment was wasted. During meals and the bath books were read to him while he took notes; when on the move he dictated to a secretary. The only work to survive is his 37-volume *Natural History*, a rather superficial encyclopaedia of geography and the natural sciences.

NATURAL HISTORY, 4:9-11

The Peloponnese, which was previously called Apia and Pelasgia, is a peninsula inferior in celebrity to no region of the earth. It lies between two seas, the Aegean and the Ionian, and resembles in shape the leaf of a plane-tree; on account of the angular indentations the circuit of its coast-line, according to Isidore, amounts to 563 miles, and nearly as much again in addition, measuring the shores of the bays.

The narrow neck of land from which it projects is called the Isthmus. At this place the two seas that have been mentioned encroach on opposite sides from the north and east and swallow up all the breadth of the peninsula at this point, until in consequence of the inroad of such large bodies of water in opposite directions the coasts on either side have been eaten away so as to leave a space between them of only five miles, with the result that the Morea is only attached to Greece by a narrow neck of land. The inlets on either side are called the Gulf of Corinth and the Saronic Gulf, the former ending in Lechaeum and the latter in Cenchreae. The circuit of the Morea is a long and dangerous voyage for vessels prohibited by their size from being carried across the Isthmus on trolleys, and consequently successive attempts were made by King Demetrius, Caesar the dictator and the emperors Caligula and Nero, to dig a ship-canal through the narrow part — an undertaking which the end that befell them all proves to have been an act of sacrilege.

In the middle of this neck of land which we have called the Isthmus is the colony of Corinth, the former name of which was Ephyra; its habitations cling to the side of a hill, 7½ miles from the coast on either side, and the top of its citadel, called Acrocorinth, on which is the spring of Peirene, commands views of the two seas in opposite directions.

The graphic description of the Peloponnese as a broad-bladed leaf hanging from the underside of Greece (cf. fig. 1) highlights the importance of the stem attaching it to the mainland. Only 7 kms wide it denied seafarers an alternative to the fearsome channel between Cape Malea and the island of Cythera (see Strabo, p. 53 above). Hence, as early as the 6th cent. B.C. the question of cutting a canal linking the Corinthian and Saronic Gulfs was mooted. Diogenes Laertius (early 3rd cent. A.D.) says that Periander (c. 625-585 B.C.) "wanted to dig a canal through the Isthmus" (1:99). The project came to nothing. The next attempt was made by Demetrius I, Poliorcetes, of Macedonia (336-283 B.C.); for the reasons why he never even got started see Strabo, p. 52 above. Inevitably the plan resurfaced when Julius Caesar refounded Corinth in 44 B.C. (see Suetonius, p. 114 below); it was again proposed by Gaius Caligula (see Suetonius). In both cases the project was abandoned without any work being done because of the deaths of the two rulers. The only one to actually make a start was Nero (for details see Suetonius) towards the end of A.D. 66. The actual canal was begun in 1881 and officially opened in 1893.

In the absence of a canal the only possibility was transshipment. Not only goods but even ships were carried across the Isthmus on the paved road called the *diolkos* (for details, see Strabo, p. 63 above). Pliny explicitly notes that many ships were too heavy to be transported in this way. Owners of such ships, who wished to avoid the dangerous voyage to the south had no alternative but to off-load at the ports of Lechaeum or Cenchreae (cf. fig. 1) and to have their cargos carried across to the other port. What we know of the ancient road system (Wiseman, 1978:64) would seem to indicate that all this traffic passed through Corinth. Not only did this generate employment, but the city certainly levied a transit tax on such goods. When measured against the risks of the southern voyage it was cheap insurance.

NATURAL HISTORY, 34:1, 6-8

1. Let our next subject be ores, etc., of copper and bronze the metals which in point of utility have the next value; in fact Corinthian bronze is valued before silver and almost even before gold....

6. Of the bronze which was renowned in early days, the Corinthian is the most highly praised. This is a compound that was produced by accident, when Corinth was burned at the time of its capture; and there has been a wonderful mania among many people for possessing this metal — in fact it is recorded that Verres, whose conviction Marcus Cicero had procured, was, together with Cicero, proscribed by Antony for no other reason than because he had refused to give up to Antony some pieces of Corinthian ware. To me the majority of these collectors seem only to make a pretence of being connoisseurs, so as to separate themselves from the multitude, rather than to have any exceptionally refined insight in this matter; and this I will briefly show.

7. Corinth was taken in the third year of the 158th Olympiad, which was the 608th year of our city, when for ages

there had no longer been any famous artists in metal-work; yet these persons designate all the specimens of their work as Corinthian bronzes. In order therefore to refute them we will state the periods to which these artists belong; of course it will be easy to turn the Olympiads into the years since the foundation of our city by referring to the two corresponding dates given above.

8. The only genuine Corinthian vessels are then those which your connoisseurs sometimes convert into dishes for food and sometimes into lamps or even washing basins, without regard for the neatness of the workman-ship. There are three kinds of this sort of bronze: a white variety, coming very near to silver in brilliance, in which the alloy of silver predominates; a second kind, in which the yellow quality of gold predominates; and a third kind, in which all the metals were blended in equal proportions. Besides these there is another mixture the formula for which cannot be given, although it is man's handiwork. But the bronze valued in portrait statues and others for its peculiar colour, approaching the appearance of liver and consequently called by a Greek name *hepatizon* meaning 'liverish,' is a blend produced by luck. It is far behind the Corinthian blend, yet a long way in front of the bronze of Aegina and that of Delos which long held the first rank.

This account is marked by a certain incoherence, not to say inconsistency. Pliny first suggests that Corinthian bronze first came into existence in 146 B.C. when Corinth was burnt, giving the impression that vessels somehow changed colour in the fire. Taken in this sense the theory is implausible. The vessels would have melted. In this case we might suppose that Corinthian ware was a creation of the post-44 B.C. Roman settlers who used the fused metal found in the ruins. This hypothesis, however, is excluded, and Pliny's initial suggestion refuted, by his own insistence that the artists who produced Corinthian bronze had been long dead by 146 B.C. The promised list of these artists and their dates is not given, and we can only assume that he had in mind the list of Greek artists in bronze given in *NH*,

34:49-52, for there he claims that there were no really great artists after the 121st Olympiad (296-293 B.C.).

Genuine Corinthian bronze, according to Pliny, is not monumental; it appears in objects which can be used as dishes, basins, and lamps (cf. Petronius, p. 85 above). Since he insists that "it is admitted that there are no lampstands made of Corinthian metal" (*NH*, 34:12), we must conclude that the objects converted into lamps were figurines.

Pliny's distinction of four different types of alloy is not based on metallurgical analysis, but on observation. The objects which he was prepared to accept as of Corinthian origin differed in color. Consciously or unconsciously he was influenced by the monetary value of the objects, and so articulated the modulations in terms of different proportions of precious metals, notably gold and silver. This interpretation is confirmed by the fact that he can offer no explanation for the fourth color. By focusing on gold and silver he can produce only three combinations. He could have explained the fourth type by postulating a preponderance of copper, but this would have conflicted with his assumption of intrinsic value.

Although no Corinthian bronzes are known (Pemberton), the effects of blending gold and silver into copper have been studied. According to Craddock, parallels would suggest that Corinthian bronze should be understood as a family of surface-treated alloys to which allusions appear in the work of the alchemists. Following Caley, he points out that since cold water cannot be used to temper bronze, as Pausanias claims (p. 29 above), the flow from the Peirene fountain may have been used in the preparation of solutions in which the alloys were treated.

NATURAL HISTORY, 34:48

> Owners of the figurines called Corinthian are usually so enamoured of them that they carry them about with them; for instance the orator Hortensius was never parted from the sphinx which he had got out of Verres when on trial. This explains Cicero's retort when Hortensius in the course of an altercation at the trial in question

said that he was no good at riddles. "You ought to be," said Cicero, "since you keep a sphinx at home!" The emperor Nero also used to carry about with him an Amazon which we shall describe later, and a little before Nero, the ex-consul Gaius Cestius used to go about with a sphinx which he had with him even on the battlefield.

The possible ambiguity of 'called' is resolved by Quintillian's witness that the sphinx of Hortensius was of bronze (*Institutio Oratorica*, 6:3.98), and by the subsequent reference to Nero's Amazon, "Strongylion made an Amazon, which from the remarkable beauty of the legs is called the Eucnemon, which consequently the emperor Nero caused to be carried in his retinue on his journeys" (*NH*, 34:82). Strongylion was an artist of the mid-5th cent. B.C. and, apart from one group of muses, all his statues were in bronze (PW, 4/A1:372). This is the only Corinthian figurine attributed to a specific artist. Martial mentions two further figurines, Apollo watching a lizard (*Epigrams*, 14:172) and the infant Hercules throttling two snakes (*Epigrams*, 14:177).

Despite the impression given by Pliny, it would be absurd to imagine that these figurines were small enough to go in someone's pocket; the meaning must be that they were moved whenever the owners changed residences. See the remarks below (p. 108) on the small statue acquired by his nephew.

No extant bronze figure can be attributed with certainty to Corinth (Pemberton: 109); for a synthetic treatment of the whole question see Murphy-O'Connor, 1983.

JOSEPHUS

According to his autobiography (*Life*) Josephus was born in the first year of Caligula's reign (A.D. 37-38) and survived into the last years of the 1st cent. A.D. After an unimpressive two-year military career as one of the leaders of the

Jewish forces in Galilee (A.D. 66-67), he was taken prisoner by the Romans, but won the favour of the emperor Vespasian, who gave him citizenship and a house in Rome. There he wrote *The Jewish War*, which was published in A.D. 75-79, and *The Antiquities of the Jews*, which appeared in A.D. 93-94. Shortly afterwards he composed his autobiography and *Against Appion*.

JEWISH WAR, 5:201-205

> Of the gates nine were completely overlaid with gold and silver, as were also their door-posts and lintels; but one, that outside the sanctuary, was of Corinthian bronze, and far exceeded in value those plated with silver and set in gold. Each gateway had two doors, and each door was 30 cubits in height and 15 in breadth. Beyond and within the entrances, however, the portals expanded, embracing on either side turret-like chambers measuring 30 cubits in breadth and length, and over 40 cubits high, each supported by two columns, 12 cubits in circumference. The dimensions of the other gates were all alike, but the one beyond the Corinthian gate, opening from the Womens Court on the east, opposite the gate of the sanctuary, was far larger, having an altitude of 50 cubits, with doors of 40 cubits, and richer decoration, being overlaid with massive plates of silver and gold. The nine gates were thus plated by Alexander the father of Tiberius.

This passage is taken from Josephus' description of the Temple built by Herod the Great in Jerusalem. The Corinthian gate, so called because of the origin of its bronze, is to be identified with the Nicanor Gate, because we read in the Mishnah, "All the gates that were there had been changed and overlaid with gold, save only the doors of the Nicanor Gate, for with them a miracle had happened and, some say, because their bronze shone like gold." (*Middoth*, 2:3). This text is amplified in the Talmud, "What miracles were performed by his doors? When Nicanor went to Alexandria in Egypt to bring them, on his return a huge wave threatened to engulf him. Thereupon they took one of the doors and cast it into the sea but still the sea continued to rage. When they prepared to cast the other one into the sea, Nicanor rose and clung to it, saying, 'Cast me in with it!' The sea immediately became calm. He was, however, deeply grieved about the other door. As they reached the harbour of Acre it broke the surface and appeared from under the sides of the boat. Others say a sea monster swallowed it and ejected it out on to dry land. Subsequently, all the gates of the Sanctuary were changed for golden ones, but the Nicanor gates, which were of bronze, were left because of the miracles wrought with them. But some say that they were retained because the bronze of which they were made had a golden hue. R. Eliezer b. Jacob said, 'It was Corinthian copper which shone like gold.'" (*Yoma*, 38a).

The dispute about the precise location of this gate in the Temple need not concern us here. The confirmation of what Pliny says (p. 86 above) regarding the value and colour of Corinthian bronze is important, but it is less significant than the clear implication that first-class Corinthian bronze was available in Alexandria around the middle of the 1st cent. A.D., the commonly accepted date for Nicanor (*Encyclopaedia Judaica*, 12:1134). Where did this bronze come from? No certain answer can be given, because there are at least two possibilities. The bronze industry was reestablished in Corinth by the Roman colonists of the post-44 B.C. period (Murphy-O'Connor, 1983), and so there is the possibility that raw, unformed bronze was exported to Alexandria. No ancient text, however, even hints at this type of trade. The other possibility is that bronze vessels of the pre-146 B.C. period — some are attested in Alexandria (Athenaeus, *Deipnosophistae*, 199e; cf. Murphy-O'Connor, 1983) — were melted down, the doors being fashioned by Jewish craftsmen from the raw material thus obtained. Given the value of such antiques (cf. Suetonius, p. 116 below), their destruction would be inconceivable were it not for the profound attachment of Jews to the Temple.

LIFE, 68

> I went down to Tiberias, and took all the care I could of
> the royal furniture, to recover all that could be recovered
> from such as had plundered it. They consisted of candela-
> bra of Corinthian bronze, and of royal tables, and of a
> great quantity of uncoined silver; and I resolved to pre-
> serve whatsoever came to my hand for the king.

The fact that Josephus unconsciously mentions first the
candelabra underlines the common estimation of the value
of Corinthian bronze. A Corinthian candelabrum is also mentioned by Martial (*Epigrams*, 14:43), but their authenticity
must be considered very doubtful in view of Pliny the
Elder's statement that there was a consensus that there were
no genuine Corinthian candelabra, "yet this name is commonly attached to them, because although Mummius' victory destroyed Corinth, it caused the dispersal of bronzes
from a number of the towns of Achaia at the same time"
(*NH*, 34:12).

MARTIAL

Marcus Valerius Martialis was born in Spain in c. A.D. 40
and arrived in Rome in A.D. 64. He lived in poverty for many
years, but eventually made his mark as a poet whose capacity
for precise observation and condensed expression enabled him
to offer unparalleled vignettes of all aspects of Roman life.
Pliny the Younger paid for his return to Spain in A.D. 98,
where he died six years later.

EPIGRAMS, 5:35

> While Euclides in scarlet was loudly proclaiming that two
> hundred thousand sesterces a year were the return of his

farms at Patrae, and that an even greater sum came from
his property in the suburbs of Corinth, and was tracing a
long pedigree from beauteous Leda, and arguing with Lei-
tus who was making him stir—out of the pocket of this
proud, high-born, rich knight there suddenly fell a big key.
Never, Fabullus, was there a key more wicked.

The vibrations set up by the falling key shattered the bub-
ble of Euclides' pretensions. He stood revealed as a menial
not a millionaire. The point of the epigram would be lost,
however, were not the suburbs of Corinth a recognized source
of great wealth. How they were exploited remains unclear.

DIO CHRYSOSTOM

Dio Cocceianus Chrysostomus was born c. A.D. 40 at
Prusa in Bithynia. He was won over to Stoicism by Musonius Rufus sometime after arriving in Rome during the
reign of Vespasian (A.D. 69-79), a philosophy he was forced
to live out when in A.D. 82 he was banished from Italy and
his homeland. For 14 years he wandered the empire penniless, supporting himself at times by the meanest manual
labour. In A.D. 97, the year after his exile ended, he delivered an oration at the Olympic games. Fortified by the
support of the emperor Trajan (A.D. 98-117) the last years
of his life were peaceful, and he was able to devote himself to
beautifying his native city and to propagating his philosophy in the discourses which later won for him the title
'Golden-mouthed'. He is last heard of in A.D. 112 and
probably died about A.D. 120.

DISCOURSES, 6:1-6

1. When Diogenes of Sinope was exiled from that place,
he came to Greece and used to divide his time between

Corinth and Athens. And he said that he was following the practice of the Persian king. . . .

2. So he too, he said, changed his residence according to the seasons of the year. For Attica had no high mountains, nor rivers running through it as had the Peloponnese and Thessaly; its soil was thin and the air so dry that rain rarely fell, and what did fall was not retained. Besides it was almost entirely surrounded by the sea; from which fact indeed it got its name, since Attica means a sort of beach-land. The city, moreover was low-lying and faced to the south, as shown by the fact that those sailing from Sunium could not enter Piraeus except with a south wind. Naturally, therefore, the winters were mild.

3. In Corinth, on the other hand, the summer was breezy since currents of air always met there on account of the bays that dented the shore. Acrocorinth, too, overshadows it, and the city itself rather inclines towards Lechaeum and the north.

4. Diogenes thought that these cities were far more beautiful than Ecbatana and Babylon, and that the Craneum and the Athenian acropolis with the Propylaea were far more beautiful structures than those abodes of royalty, yielding to them only in size. . . .

6. Moreover, the king had a very long distance to travel in changing residences; he had to spend pretty much the larger part of the winter and summer on the road. He himself, on the other hand, by spending the night near Megara, could very easily be in Athens on the following day — or else, if he preferred, at Eleusis; otherwise, he could take a shorter way through Salamis, without passing through any deserts.

DISCOURSES, 8:5-10

5. After Antisthenes' death Diogenes moved to Corinth, since he considered none of the others worth associating with, and there he lived without renting a house or staying with a friend, but camping out in the Craneum. For he observed that large numbers gathered at Corinth on

account of the harbours and the hetaerae, and because the city was situated as it were at the cross-roads of Greece. Accordingly, just as the good physician should go and offer his services where the sick are most numerous, so, said he, the man of wisdom should take up his abode where fools are thickest in order to convict them of their folly and reprove them.

6. So, when the time for the Isthmian games arrived, and everybody was at the Isthmus, he went down also. . . .

9. That was the time when one could hear crowds of wretched sophists around Poseidon's temple shouting and reviling one another, and their disciples, as they were called, fighting with one another, many writers reading aloud their stupid works, many poets reciting their poems while others applauded them, many jugglers showing their tricks, many fortune-tellers interpreting fortunes, lawyers innumerable perverting judgement, and peddlers not a few peddling whatever they happened to have.

10. Naturally a crowd gathered about him immediately. No Corinthians, however, for they did not think it would be at all worth their while, since they were accustomed to see him every day at Corinth. The crowd that gathered was composed of strangers.

These two excerpts belong to discourses written when Dio was a penniless wanderer. "Many of the things that Dio speaks of Diogenes doing . . . fit better the experience of Dio himself, and many of the references to the Persian king would apply just as well to Domitian, who banished Dio. No doubt the speaker's audiences would understand his veiled allusions quite easily ." (Cohoon, 1:249).

Of Diogenes' precise movements Dio would have known little, apart from the traditions which associated him with Athens and Corinth. The details of the climate of the two cities is certainly accurate, and the vividness of the description of Corinth sloping down from Acrocorinth to the sea betrays an eyewitness. Dio is equally precise regarding the routes to Athens. The ferry from Cenchreae would naturally touch at the island of Salamis before going on to Piraeus.

The alternative was the land route. Megara is 40 kms from Corinth, and Athens a further 42 kms, both average hikes for walkers of the period (cf. Jewett: 139). An overnight at Eleusis is rightly put as a less preferable alternative, because it would mean a first-day hike of 60 kms; not impossible but one would want to be in very good shape. Finally, Craneum was the most beautiful spot in Corinth (cf. Pausanias, p. 22 above).

Thus, it appears highly probable that when Dio describes the crowd scene at Isthmia he is again reflecting personal experience. It is this sort of vivid cameo that brings to life the wild excitement of that great gathering. The games were, of course, the focal point, but many other things were going on as well (cf. p. 14 above). First-hand knowledge is also evidenced by the observation that the victor's crown at the Isthmian games was of celery (cf. Plutarch, p. 102 below), "The noble man holds his hardships to be his greatest antagonists, and with them he is ever wont to battle day and night, not to win a sprig of celery, as so many goats might do, nor for a bit of wild olive or of pine, but to win happiness and virtue throughout all the days of his life, and not merely when the Eleans [Olympic games] make proclamation, or the Corinthians [Isthmian games], or the Thessalians assemble [Pythian games]." (8:15).

Some of the language in this last citation immediately evokes 1 Cor 9:25, and it is far from improbable that the reason which made Paul center his ministry in Corinth was the same that motivated Diogenes/Dio.

DISCOURSES, 31:103 and 121

> 103. .... It is not possible to compare all that which may now be seen in our time, when you appear with merely one or two undecked ships every year at Corinth....
>
> 121. .... In regard to the gladiatorial shows the Athenians have so zealously emulated the Corinthians, or rather, have so surpassed both them and all others in their mad infatuation, that, whereas the Corinthians watch these combats outside the city in a glen, a place that is able to

> hold a crowd but otherwise is dirty and such that no one
> would even bury there any freeborn citizen, the Athen-
> ians look on at this fine spectacle in their theatre under
> the very walls of the Acropolis....

This discourse is thought to be made up of two distinct speeches both addressed to the people of Rhodes, one delivered in the early years of the reign of Vespasian (A.D. 69-79), the other under Titus (A.D. 79-81) (Cohoon, 3:4).

The point of mentioning the two ships is to contrast the past and present of Rhodes in terms of sea-power, but the sharpness of the observation — they were 'undecked' — would again seem to betray eye-witness knowledge. Could Dio have passed through Cenchreae on his way to Rome? It would have been the easiest route from Asia (cf. Philostratus, p. 130 below).

The site of the amphitheatre is noted in fig. 4. It has not been excavated but the configuration of the terrain makes the identification certain. When seen by Dio it was apparently only a natural depression, without any buildings, but which nonetheless served as a makeshift arena for gladiatorial shows. The Corinthians, therefore, would have had little trouble visualising what Paul meant when he said he had fought with beasts (1 Cor 15:32). The site was within the walls, so when Dio says that it was 'outside the city' we must understand this as meaning that it was in an open space between the built-up area and the walls. On the basis of what we have already noted with regard to Pausanias (p. 22 above), it would seem that any housing on the east side of 1st cent. Corinth was of very low density. The presence of cemeteries elsewhere would also indicate that only at rare points did the city approach the girdle wall (Carpenter: 346).

DISCOURSES, 37:8 and 36

> 8. However, in my own case, upon my second visit to
> Corinth you were so glad to see me that you did your best
> to get me to stay with you, but seeing that to be impossi-
> ble, you did have a likeness made of me, and you took this

and set it up in your Library, a front-row seat as it were, where you felt it would most effectively stimulate the youth to persevere in the same pursuits as myself. For you accorded me this honour, not as to one of the many who each year put in at Cenchreae as traders or pilgrims or envoys or passing travellers, but as to a cherished friend, who at last, after a long absence, puts in an appearance....

36....You are now, as the saying goes, both prow and stern of Hellas, having been called prosperous and wealthy and the like by poets and gods from olden days, days when some of the others too had wealth and might; but now, since wealth has deserted both Orchomenos and Delphi, though they may surpass you in exciting pity, none can do so in exciting envy.

This discourse, addressed to the Corinthians, has long been recognized as spurious. It is attributed to Favorinus (c. A.D. 80-150). He studied under Dio Chrysostom, and taught Herod the Athenian, one of the great 2nd cent. A.D. benefactors of Corinth (cf. Pausanias, p. 10 above). Plutarch was one of his friends. He may have visited Corinth when exiled from Rome to the island of Chios.

Building n. 34 in fig. 5 has been suggested as a probable candidate for the Library (Wiseman, 1979:514); it was erected shortly after the founding of the Roman colony in 44 B.C. The emphasis on the prosperity of Corinth, which excited the envy of other Greek cities, explains why the merchant is mentioned first in the list of visitors to Cenchreae, the eastern port of Corinth (fig. 1). Since the pilgrim is contrasted with the passing traveller it seems logical to conclude that Corinth was his goal; the reference is probably to those who represented their cities at the Isthmian festivals. Mention of envoys underlines the political influence of Corinth which was the inevitable concomitant of its economic power. Finally, the evocation of passing travellers points up the position of Corinth as the cross-roads of the eastern Mediterranean.

PLUTARCH

Plutarch would have been a very small boy when Paul was ministering at Corinth. The date of his birth is not certain; it was certainly before A.D. 50 and the figure commonly given is A.D. 46 or 47. He came from a prominent and wealthy family of Chaeroneia, a small town located some 65 kms due north of Corinth on the far side of the Corinthian Gulf and about 35 kms due east of Delphi. His studies at the Platonic Academy in Athens (c. A.D. 66) made him one of the best educated men of his age, and his life of study, lecturing and writing was interrupted only by the demands of civic and religious duty. His immense literary production is classified under two headings. The *Moralia* comprise 28 ethical, religious, physical, political and religious studies, whereas the *Lives* are biographies of 50 Greek and Roman soldiers and statesmen. He died c. A.D. 120.

Though widely travelled, he retained Chaeroneia as his permanent base lest through his leaving it should become even smaller (Ziegler: 657). His writings contain two specific references to visits to Corinth, but it is likely that there were others. As a young man he was sent on a mission to the Proconsul of Achaia (*Moralia*, 816D) whose capital was Corinth; the evidence is not as clear as one would wish but Apuleius (born c. A.D. 123) calls Corinth "the head of the whole province of Achaia" (*Metamorphoses*, 10:18). Moreover, Plutarch made at least two trips to Rome, one towards the end of the 70's and the other at the beginning of the 90's (Ziegler: 656), and Corinth would have been a natural staging point (cf. Philostratus, p. 130 below). We can safely assume that Plutarch was an eye-witness of first century Corinth.

QUAESTIONES CONVIVIALES, 5:3.1-3 (675D-677B)

1. The pine, and why it was used for the crown at the Isthmian games, was the subject of a discussion at a

dinner given us in Corinth itself during the games by Lucanius, the chief priest. Praxiteles, the official guide, appealed to mythology, citing the legend that the body of Melicertes was found cast up by the sea at the foot of a pine. . . .

2. On hearing these remarks, a professor of rhetoric, who was reputed to have a wider acquaintance with polite literature than anyone else, said, "In heaven's name! Wasn't it only yesterday or the day before that the pine became the garland of victory at the Isthmia? Formerly it was celery. This is evident from the comedy where a miser says: 'I'd gladly sell the entire Isthmian show for the price at which the celery crown will go.' . . . ."

3. . . . It seems to me that I have also read a passage on the Isthmia by Procles, in which the author records that the first contest was held for a crown of pine, but that later, when the contest was made sacred, they adopted the celery crown from the Nemean games.

QUAESTIONES CONVIVIALES,
8:4.1 and 5 (723A and 724F)

1. During the Isthmian games, the second time Sospis was president, I avoided the other banquets, at which he entertained a great many foreign visitors at once, and several times entertained all the citizens. Once, however, when he entertained in his home his closest friends, all men of learning, I was present too. At the clearing away of the first course, someone came in to present Herodes the professor of rhetoric, as a special honour, with palm-frond and a plaited wreath sent by a pupil who had won a contest with an encomiastic oration. After accepting them, he sent them back again, remarking that he did not understand why, of the various games, each one has as prize a different kind of wreath, but all use the palm-frond. . . .

5. . . . (Caphisias says) "If you impose weight on a piece of palm wood, it does not bend down and give way, but curves up in the opposite direction, as though resisting

him who would force it. This is the way with athletic contests, too. Those who cannot stand the strain because of weakness and softness are pressed down and forced to bend, but those who stoutly bear up under training are raised up and exalted, not in body only but in mind as well."

Without being a verbatim stenographic record Plutarch's 'Table Discussions' are considered to be records of genuine conversations that took place at specific places and times with real persons, his friends and contemporaries (Ziegler: 886-887). Thus we can date at least one of Plutarch's visits to Corinth, because his host, Antonius Sospis, is known from two inscriptions found at Corinth to have been president of the Isthmian games three times during the reign of Trajan (A.D. 98-117) (Kent: 78-79). Thus, the visit should be placed in the first decade of the 2nd cent. A.D. This conclusion is confirmed by the dedication of the essay *De capienda ex inimicis utilitate* (*Moralia*, 86B) to Cornelius Pulcher who is known, again from a series of inscriptions, to have played an eminent role in the civic life of Corinth in the time of Trajan (Kent: 64-65). A passing reference at the end of the introduction to this work is not without significance; the author claims to have omitted "matter contained in my *Advice to Statesmen* since I observe that you often have that book close at hand" (86D). This rather smug remark would make it appear that Plutarch was a frequent visitor to Corinth, presumably on the occasion of the great panhellenic festival, the Isthmian games. The crisp spring days would have been spent in the sanctuary of Poseidon (cf. p. 10) above) participating in the rites and watching the contests. In the evening he would have returned to the city to discuss late into the night in the homes of his eminent friends, some of them almost certainly located in Craneum (cf. p. 22 above).

The discussion regarding the composition of the Isthmian victory crown is relevant to 1 Cor 9:25 because it conveys a very accurate picture of what actually occurred. The available textual and monumental evidence has been collected by O. Broneer who concludes that pine was used from the foundation of the games to the early 5th cent. B.C. when celery was substituted — the scholia on Pindar, *Olympian* 3:27 and *Isthmian* 2:19 insist that it was withered as opposed to the fresh celery of the Nemean crown — only to give way to pine once again towards the end of the 1st cent. A.D. (1962a).

The benefits of training, as articulated at the end of the second quotation, are echoed by Paul in 1 Cor 9:24-27.

QUAESTIONES CONVIVIALES, 6:10.1 (696E)

> 1. Aristion's cook made a hit with the dinner guests not only because of his general skill, but because the cock that he set before the diners, though it had just been slaughtered as a sacrifice to Heracles, was as tender as if it had been a day old. Aristion said that meat cures rapidly if, immediately upon killing, it is hung on a fig tree; and we went on to discuss why this should be so.

There is no evidence that this episode occurred in Corinth, but the situation is that evoked by Paul in 1 Cor 10:27-30 where a guest is offered meat sacrificed to idols. Meat was not a normal part of the dinner menu, and was generally available only on the occasion of sacrifices (Smith: 12).

SEPTEM SAPIENTIUM CONVIVIUM, 2 and 3 (146DE and 148B)

> 2. Periander had arranged for the entertainment, not in the city, but in the dining-hall in the vicinity of Lechaeum, close by the shrine of Aphrodite, in whose honour the sacrifice was offered that day. . . .
>
> For each of the invited guests a carriage and pair, fasionably caparisoned, was brought to the door; for it was summer-time, and the whole length of the street even to the water's edge was one mass of dust and confusion by reason of the great crowd of vehicles and people. Thales, however, when he saw the equipage at the door, smiled

> and dismissed it. And so we set out on foot, leaving the road and going through the fields in a leisurely fashion....
>
> 3. Engaging in such discourse as this along the way, we arrived at the house. Thales did not care to bathe, for we had already had a rub-down. So he visited and inspected the race-tracks, the training-quarters of the athletes, and the beautifully kept park along the shore....

The Dinner of the Seven Wise Men is a purely imaginary work in which Plutarch records the table-conversation of figures of the 6th cent. B.C. The scene is set in the port of Lechaeum (cf. p. 19 above) and it is not impossible that, in order to lend added piquancy to his account, Plutarch described the Lechaeum of his day. Certainly the Lechaeum Road would have been exactly as he depicts it, and the 2.5 km walk in the open outside the Long Walls (cf. fig. 4) would not have been beyond the capacity of gentlemen of his class. However, since virtually no archaeological work has been done at Lechaeum, the existence of the buildings mentioned cannot be verified.

There is no reason why Plutarch should not have known Lechaeum. The most comfortable way for him to have come to the Isthmian games from his home at Chaeroneia would have been by boat from Cirrha (modern Kirra 2.5 kms east of Itea), the port of Delphi (Pausanias, 20:37.4), or Antikyra (modern Andikira) in the next bay to the east. Equally, on route to Rome from Athens he would have sailed from Piraeus to Cenchreae, crossed the Isthmus on foot, and taken ship again from Lechaeum (cf. Philostratus, p. 130 below).

APOTHEGMATA LACONICA (221F)

> Thorycion, arriving from Delphi and seeing in the Isthmus the forces of Philip, who had already gained possession of the narrow entrance, said, "The Peloponnese has poor gate-keepers in you, men of Corinth!"

The remark of the Spartan general underlines the immense strategic importance of Corinth. Its situation enabled it to control access to the Peloponnese from the north. Crucial in military terms, it was an even greater advantage economically (cf. Strabo, p. 55 above).

DE PYTHIAE ORACULIS, 2 (395B-D)

The guides were going through their prearranged programme, paying no heed to us who begged that they would cut short their harangues and their expounding of most of the inscriptions. The appearance and technique of the statues had only a moderate attraction for the foreign visitor, who, apparently, was a connoisseur in works of art. He did, however, admire the patina of the bronze, for it bore no resemblance to verdigris or rust, but the bronze was smooth and shining with a deep blue tinge, so that it gave an added touch to the sea-captains (for he had begun his sight-seeing at this point), as they stood there with the true complexion of the sea and in its deepest depths.

"Was there, then," he said, "some process of alloying and treating used by the artizans of early times for bronze, something like what is called the tempering of swords, on the disappearance of which bronze came to have a respite from employment in war? As a matter of fact," he continued, "it was not by art, as they say, but by accident that the Corinthian bronze acquired its beauty of colour; a fire consumed a house containing some gold and silver and a great store of copper, and when these were melted and fused together, the great mass of copper furnished a name because of its preponderance."

Theon, taking up the conversation, said, "We have heard another more artful account, how a worker in bronze at Corinth, when he had come upon a hoard containing much gold, fearing detection, broke it off a little at a time and stealthily mixed it with his bronze, which thus acquired a wondrous composition. He sold it for a goodly price since it was very highly esteemed for its colour and beauty. However, both this story and that are fiction, but there was apparently some process of combination and preparation; for even now they alloy gold with silver and produce a peculiar and extraordinary, and, to my eyes, a sickly paleness and an unlovely perversion."

In the 1st cent. A.D. Corinthian bronzes were considered collector's items (cf. Pliny the Younger, p. 108 below); the fad had reached such proportions that it was mocked by the satirists (cf. Petronius, p. 84 above). It was inevitable, therefore, that there should be discussion as to what gave it its specific character. The interminable professional guides at Delphi (the sort of people on whom Pausanias relied for local information) obviously had no answer. Pausanias' own suggestion (p. 30 above) has little more merit than the legends recorded, and dismissed, here. They do, however, underline that the colour of Corinthian bronze was quite different to the deep blue of the statues of the sea-captains, presumably the 37 statues of Lysander and his officers which stood just inside the entrance to the sanctuary of Delphi. The emphasis on gold suggests that it was a ruddy colour; for more detail see the discussion by Pliny the Elder (p. 88 above). Note the possible implication that bronze was still being made at Corinth (cf. Pausanias, p. 31 above).

DE VITANDO AERE ALIENO, 7 (831A)

And so 'one after another takes over' the borrower, first an usurer or broker of Corinth, then one of Patrae, then an Athenian, until, attacked on all sides by all of them, he is dissolved and chopped up into the small change of interest payments. For just as a man who has fallen into the mire must either get up or stay where he is, but he who turns and rolls over covers his wet and drenched person with more dirt; so in their transfers and changes of loans, by assuming additional interest payments and plastering themselves with them, they weigh themselves down more and more.

The reference to Corinth here is only incidental, but it is all the more important in that it is unconscious. That Plutarch instinctively mentions Corinth, Patrae and Athens when thinking of borrowing and interest indicates that they were the three great banking centers of Roman Greece. It is equally significant that he puts Corinth at the head of the list, before Patrae (modern Patras) to the west outside the narrows of the Corinthian Gulf and Athens to the east. Its immense importance as a trade center would have demanded the development of banking facilities but, curiously, this is the only ancient text to allude to this function. Plutarch's remark should not be taken to mean that Corinth, Patrae, and Athens were especially usurious; what little evidence there is would suggest that interest rates ranged from 4% to 12% (Larsen: 491).

AMATORIUS, 21 (767F)

You have, of course, heard of Laïs, the theme of song, the essence of loveliness — how she threw all Greece into a fever of longing or was, rather, the object of contention from sea to sea. But when she fell in love with Hippolochus the Thessalian, "Forsaking Acrocorinth bathed in grey-green water," (Euripides) and escaping secretly from the vast throngs of her other lovers and from the great army of harlots, she beat an orderly retreat. But when she came to Thessaly, the women there were envious and jealous of her beauty, decoyed her into a temple of Aphrodite, and stoned her to death.

DE HERODOTI MALIGNITATE, 39 (871A-C)

The Corinthian women were the only women in Greece who offered that splendid inspired prayer that the goddess should fire their husbands with a passionate love for battle with the barbarian; it is incredible that a man like Herodotus should be unaware of this; even the remotest Carian must have heard of it, because the story was in everyone's mouth and Simonides wrote an epigram for the bronze statues that were set up in the temple of Aphrodite (the temple which Medea is supposed to have established, according to one version when she found herself no longer in love with her husband, according to another to thank the goddess for curing Jason of his love for Thetis). This is the epigram: "Here stand those ladies who to Cypris prayed for Greece and for our stalwart fighting men. The gods were with them; Aphrodite vowed our stronghold should not fail to Persian bows." Here is something that he should have recorded — here is something worth remembering — instead of dragging in the sorry tale of Ameinocles killing his son.

Both of these passages have in common the association of love with Acrocorinth. The story of Laïs, dated in the 5th cent. B.C. by the mention of Nicias, has been told above (p. 21) by Pausanias. At first sight what is said here would appear to confirm the account of Strabo (p. 56 above), but this is not in fact the case. Not only is there no hint that Laïs functioned in the temple of Aphrodite, but Acrocorinth here stands for the city. Thus 'the great army of harlots' is a reference to city prostitutes and not to the servants of Aphrodite.

The importance of the second passage is that it provides the correct understanding for the epigram from which Athenaeus (p. 132 below) drew a completely false conclusion. The occasion was the Persian invasion of 480 B.C. and the ladies were virtuous matrons whose statues, not they themselves (as Athenaeus suggests), were placed in the temple of Aphrodite on Acrocorinth.

LIFE OF CAESAR, 47:8

And in the effort to surround himself with men's good will as the fairest and at the same time the securest protection, he again courted the people with banquets and distributions of grain, and his soldiers with newly planted colonies, the most conspicuous of which were Carthage and Corinth. The earlier capture of both these

cities, as well as their present restoration chanced to fall
at one and the same time.

This text is so condensed that it risks giving the false
impression that Corinth was settled by veterans. This is
contradicted by Strabo (p. 68 above) but can possibly be
reconciled with Appian (p. 117 below). However, contradic-
tions should not be forced, and it is possible that Plutarch
wanted to say (a) that Caesar founded colonies of which
some were staffed by veterans — in fact in 45-44 B.C. he
founded at least 18 colonies outside Italy (PW 4:526-533)
—and (b) that Carthage and Corinth were the greatest of all
the colonies he founded, as they certainly were at the time of
Plutarch.

JUVENAL

Nothing certain is known about the career of Decimus Iunius
Iuvenalis, the greatest of the Roman satirists, but vague and
often ambiguous hints have been combined to produce the following picture. Born c. A.D. 55 in Aquinum to a comforta-
bly placed family, he saw military service in Britain, but
incurred the ire of the emperor Domitian (A.D. 51-96) and
c. 93 was exiled to Upper Egypt. The accession of Nerva won
him release, but he returned to Rome without career or money.
Too proud to work, he lived the squalid and humiliating life
of a penniless hanger-on until the emperor Hadrian (A.D.
76-138) granted him a pension and a small estate. Between
c. 110 and 130 he published five books of *Satires* in which
precise observation fuels his dissection of folly, meanness, vul-
garity, and vice.

SATIRES 8:112-131

Perhaps you despise the unwarlike Rhodians, the scented
sons of Corinth — and rightly so; what harm can ever be-

fall you from youths who put on perfume and shave their legs to the crutch? But steer clear of rugged Spain, give a very wide berth to Gaul and the coast of Illyria. . . . Take care not to victimize courageous, desperate men . . . the plundered keep their weapons. . . .

    If your staff are upright and honest — no long-haired catamite who can fix your verdicts for cash — if your wife is above suspicion, . . . then you can trace your lineage back to Picus.

The eight satire belongs to Book III, which is dated between A.D. 118 and 120 (Green, 14, whose translation is cited). It is addressed to a young Roman going out to govern his first province. Juvenal assures him that he would have no trouble should he exploit those as weak as the effeminate Corinthians, but that he should walk much more carefully with tougher peoples. The satirist's estimation of the Corinthians is based on his conviction that all hard-working, intelligent Greeks were in Rome, infiltrating its institutions and corrupting its values (*Satires,* 3:58-113). There were so many of them that, in his view, Corinth and Rhodes could only be populated by the effete and inept. The power of the Greeks was rooted in their commercial ability, and in the third century Rhodes rivaled Corinth as a trading center.

The reference to "a long-haired catamite" underlines the fact that in the first century A.D. long hair identified the male homosexual. All women, for example, were excluded from a ritual in which one of the participants had "his long luxuriant curls caught up in a golden hairnet" (*Satires,* 2:96). On those who tried to hide their sexual orientation Juvenal comments, "Such creatures talk in clipped, laconic style, and crop their hair crew-cut fashion, as short as their eyebrows. I prefer the perverted eunuch priest of the Mother Goddess, at least he's open and honest about it" (*Satires,* 2:14-16). Apuleius' vivid description of these priests emphasizes their long hair (*Metamorphoses,* 8:24-27). Similar references are to be found scattered throughout Greek and Latin literature (Murphy-O'Connor, 1980:485-87). It is only against this background that we can understand Paul's statement, "Does not nature itself teach you that for a man to wear long hair is degrading to him?" (1 Cor 11:14). The point at issue in the much-disputed passage 1 Cor 11:2-16 is not the position of women in the church but the differentiation between the sexes (Murphy-O'Connor, 1988).

PLINY THE YOUNGER

C. Plinius Caecilius Secundus, the nephew of Pliny the Elder, was born in A.D. 61 or 62. He became an eminent lawyer, and filled a number of posts in the public service before being named a *consul suffectus* in A.D. 100. For two years around A.D. 112 he was imperial legate in Bithynia, where he organized the persecution of Christians (*Letters*, 10:96-97). The first nine books of his correspondence date from the years A.D. 97-109 and were written, or rewritten, for publication.

LETTERS, 3:6
To Annius Severus

I have lately purchased with a legacy that was left me, a statue of Corinthian bronze. It is small, but pleasing, and finely executed, at least, if I have any taste; which most certainly in matters of this sort, as perhaps in all others, is extremely defective. However, I think even I have enough to discover the beauties of this figure; as it is naked, the faults, if there be any, as well as the perfections, are more observable.

It represents an old man in a standing posture. The bones, the muscles, the veins, and wrinkles are so strongly expressed, that you would imagine the figure to be animated. The hair is thin and failing, the forehead broad, the face shrivelled, the throat lank, the arms languid, the

breast fallen, and the belly sunk; and the back view gives the same impression of old age.

It appears to be a genuine antique, alike from its tarnish and from what remains of the original colour of the bronze. In short it is a performance so highly finished as to fix the attention of artists, and delight the least knowing observer; and this induced me, who am a mere novice in this art, to buy it. But I did so, not with any intent of placing it in my house (for I have as yet no Corinthian bronzes there) but with the design of fixing it in some conspicuous place in my native province, preferably in the temple of Jupiter; for it is a present well worthy of a temple and a god.

Pray, then, undertake this, as readily as you do all my commissions, and give immediate orders for a pedestal to be made. I leave the choice of the marble to you, but let my name be graven upon it, and if you think proper, my titles. . . .

This is the most detailed description we have of a reputed Corinthian bronze, and the enthusiastic tone indicates that the author was in danger of falling victim to a passion that was bitingly dismissed by Seneca who wrote in A.D. 49, "Would you say that a man is truly human who arranges with finical care his Corinthian bronzes, that the mania of a few makes costly, and spends the greater part of each day upon rusty bits of copper?" (*De Brevitate Vitae*, 12:2). The word 'mania' was also used by his uncle (p. 86 above).

Though the adjective 'small' is used, it should not be pressed too hard. The amount of detail, when taken in conjunction with the plan for an inscribed marble pedestal in a public place, indicates that we should think in terms of half-lifesize; certain statues in the forum at Rome in the 3rd cent. B.C. were only a meter high (Pliny, *Natural History*, 34:24).

SUETONIUS

Little is known about the personal life of Gaius Suetonius Tranquillus, and even the dates of his birth and death are uncertain (c. A.D. 69-140). He took no part in public life, except for two years when he was one of the secretaries of the emperor Hadrian (A.D. 117-138). His *Lives of the Caesars* published in A.D. 120, impartially reports the views of both their friends and enemies. The value of the opinions are untested, but Suetonius betrays no personal bias.

JULIUS, 44.

> In particular, for the adornment and convenience of the City, also for the protection and extension of the Empire, he formed more projects and more extensive ones every day; . . . to cut a canal through the Isthmus; . . . All these enterprises and plans were cut short by his death.

GAIUS, 21

> He had planned, besides, to rebuild the palace of Polycrates at Samos, to finish the temple of the Didymaean Apollo at Ephesus, but, above all, to dig a canal through the Isthmus in Greece, and he had already sent a chief centurion to survey the work.

NERO, 19

> In Achaia he attempted to cut through the Isthmus and called together the praetorians and urged them to begin the work; then at a signal given on a trumpet he was first to break ground with a mattock and to carry off a basketful of earth upon his shoulders.

The fact that Julius Caesar thought of digging the Corinthian Canal underlines that he had founded the colony at Corinth for economic reasons. The reason given for the abandonment of the project is also the most natural explanation for Gaius Caligula's failure to carry out the same plan; he died too soon.

Nero's reason for going to Greece was to show off his voice in the musical contests which were an integral part of all the Greek games. Even though his voice was "weak and husky" (*Nero*, 20), the emperor took pains that he should be listened to, for Suetonius reports, "While he was singing no one was allowed to leave the theatre even for the most urgent reasons. And so it is said that some women gave birth to children there, while many who were worn out with the listening and applauding, secretly leaped from the wall, since the gates at the entrance were closed, or feigned death and were carried out as if for burial." (*Nero*, 23). Naturally, he won first prize everywhere.

He appeared at the Isthmian games in the spring of A.D. 67 (*Nero*, 24) but, given his refusal to let affairs of state distract him from his art (*Nero*, 23), it seems unlikely that he initiated the canal project. It is more probable that the suggestion came from the merchant aristocracy of Corinth. A little flattery would easily have persuaded Nero to make a gesture signifying imperial favour and thus guaranteeing some measure at least of financial support. The fact that the city never took an independent initiative regarding the canal can only mean that the project was beyond its resources, vast as they were.

Work on the canal certainly continued throughout A.D. 67 for in September of that year the Jewish historian reports that, after suppressing the revolt in Galilee, Vespasian penned the Jewish prisoners in the stadium at Tiberias, where "of the young men, he chose 6000 of the strongest, and sent them to Nero, to dig through the Isthmus" (*Jewish War*, 3:540). Traces of the work done (cf. Pausanias, p. 9 above and Gerster's plan in Wiseman, 1978:49) reveal how seriously the project was taken. A great amount was actually accomplished before a revolt in the West and shortage of cash forced Nero to abandon it (cf. Philostratus, p. 130 below).

CLAUDIUS, 25

> He restored to the senate the provinces of Achaia and
> Macedonia, which Tiberius had taken into his own
> charge.

On the distinction between senatorial and imperial provinces, see Strabo (p. 71 above), who also shows that Achaia
was a senatorial province under Augustus. Civic protests in
A.D. 15 against bad administration forced Tiberius to attach Achaia to the imperial province of Moesia (Tacitus,
Annals, 1:76.4; 1:80.1). Its restoration by Claudius in A.D.
44 (Dio Cassius, 40:24.1) justifies the title Proconsul given to
Gallio in Acts 18:12 (cf. p. 149 below).

AUGUSTUS, 70

> He was criticized also as overfond of costly furniture and
> Corinthian bronzes and as given to gaming. Indeed, as
> early as the time of the proscriptions there was written on
> his statue, "My father concerned himself with silver, I
> with Corinthians," since it was believed that he caused
> some men to be entered in the list of the proscribed
> because of their Corinthian vases.

TIBERIUS, 34

> Complaining bitterly that the prices of Corinthian
> bronzes had risen to an immense figure and that three
> mullets had been sold for 30,000 sesterces, he proposed
> that a limit be set to household furniture and that the
> prices in the market should be regulated each year at the
> discretion of the senate.

These two texts underline the passion that Corinthian
bronzes inspired (cf. Pliny, p. 57 above). Despite the attitude of Tiberius, the imperial household had such a collection that a special bureau had to be created to take charge of
them. Inscriptions reveal that they were known as *a Corin-*

thiis or *Corinthiarii.* This, of course makes the point of the graffito on Octavian's statue; he had made himself a slave to his collector's greed.

APPIAN

No precise dates can be justified, but it is generally assumed that Appian was born around A.D. 95 and died around A.D. 165. A native of Alexandria, Egypt, where he held public office, he eventually acquired Roman citizenship and moved to Rome. The main source of his narrowly focused *Roman History* was probably an imperial annalist who wrote in the early part of the 1st cent. A.D.

HISTORY 8:136

But at a still later time it is said that Caesar, who afterwards became dictator for life ... when he was encamped near the site of Carthage, he was troubled by a dream in which he saw a whole army weeping, and that he immediately made a memorandum in writing that Carthage should be colonized. Returning to Rome not long after, and the poor asking him for land, he arranged to send some of them to Carthage and some to Corinth. But he was assassinated shortly afterward by his enemies in the Roman Senate, and his son Julius Caesar, surnamed Augustus, finding this memorandum, built the present Carthage.... Thus the Romans won the Carthaginian part of Africa, destroyed Carthage, and repeopled it again 102 years after its destruction.

This is the only text which dates the sending of colonists to Corinth by Julius Caesar (see Strabo, p. 67 above). The term here translated by 'poor' is *aporos.* The basic meaning of this adjective is 'having no way in, out, or through'; when applied to persons it can also mean 'hard to deal with, unmanageable.' The precise connotation intended by

Appian is difficult to determine. The reference could be to those who felt themselves locked into a certain social level through lack of opportunity.

However, it would be unwise to press the term too hard because the quality of Appian's information is suspect. His narrative embodies an evident contradiction which betrays either the inadequacy of his source or a failure to understand it correctly. On the one hand, he says that Julius Caesar died before he could put his plan into effect; it was actually executed by his adopted son Gaius Julius Caesar Octavianus later known as Augustus. But on the other hand, he claims that Carthage, and by implication Corinth (see Pausanias, p. 5 above) was resettled 102 years after the fall of the two cities in 146 B.C., i.e. in 44 B.C. Caesar was assassinated on the Ides of March 44 B.C. and Augustus was not in a position to do anything about colonies until the end of 43 B.C. at the earliest. Given the obvious possibility of confusion between the two Julius Caesars, it is preferable to accept the date; a round number might have been invented but the precise figure of 102 years betrays a source. Hence, Corinth was resettled before the death of Julius Caesar in 44 B.C.

Julius Caesar founded many colonies, and it is not at all impossible, as Appian suggests, that the decision to repopulate Carthage was taken during his African campaign in the first months of 46 B.C. It would also have been natural for him to have associated Corinth with it, not only because they had been destroyed in the same year but because they were intimately linked in the Roman mind on account of their strategic importance and tremendous economic potential (see Cicero, p. 48 above).

AELIUS ARISTIDES

Born at Hadriani in Mysia in A.D. 117, Publius Aelius Aristides used his family wealth to acquire the best rhetorical training available. His career as an orator was interrupted by an illness in A.D. 142, but he was cured by Asclepius and afterwards spent several years at his great shrine in Pergamum, enjoying the company of other self-centered neurasthenics. He felt sufficiently recovered to begin travel in A.D. 153 and spent time in Greece and Rome, but was stricken again when smallpox swept the empire in A.D. 165. His public appearances thereafter were fewer, and he died in A.D. 180.

ORATIONS, 46:20-31

20. For all told, if I must not involve my speech with inessentials, every shore, every harbor, every part of the earth and sea is a shrine, an offering, an image, a precinct, and a temple of Poseidon. However nothing is so dear, beloved, and honored by him as this isthmus and this region here. And I call this Poseidon's chancellery, palace, court — just as Homer spoke of "the court of Zeus" — and the headquarters of his kingdom.

21. I base my judgement, among other reasons, on the fact that he centered the whole sea on every side around this point after he had set gates on either side of it and had spread the land which is called the isthmus equally to the east and west of it, and at the same time had closed it off so that the seas might not join, not with a great expanse of land, but, as it were, with a narrow pipe, and had legislated and had ordained for the seas, that each preserve its own boundaries, 22. And again had spread them all open and had given to each a somewhat wide expanse in the distance, so that — this is the strangest and at the same time most pleasant of all the spectacles on the earth — people on each side sail in and sail out at the same instant with favorable breezes and men put out to sea and into port with the same winds in this land and sea alone of all, and everything from everywhere comes here both by land and sea, and this is the reason why the land even from the earliest times was praised as 'rich' by the poets, both

because of the multitude of advantages which are at hand and the felicity which is embodied in it.

23. For it is, as it were, a kind of market-place, and at that common to all Greeks, and a national festival, not like this present one which the Greek race celebrates here every two years, but one which is celebrated every year and daily . If, just as men enjoy the official status of being public friends with foreign cities, so too did cities enter into this relationship with one another, the city would have this title and honor everywhere. 24. For it receives all cities and sends them off again and is a common refuge for all, like a kind of route and passage for all mankind, no matter where one would travel, and it is a common city for all Greeks, indeed, as it were, a kind of metropolis and mother in this respect. For among other reasons, there is no place where one would rest as on a mother's lap with more pleasure or enjoyment. Such is the relaxation, refuge, and safety for all who come to it.

25. But so great is the abundance of beauty, desire, and love, which clings to it, that it chains all men with pleasure and all men are equally inflamed by it, which it possesses in itself "love, desire, friendly converse, and allurement so as to steal away the mind" even of those who are proud of themselves, and it has whatever else there is in addition to these, everything that is called the charms of the goddess, so that it is clearly the city of Aphrodite. And it even occurs to me to name it "the cestus," whatever this object is through which the goddess chains all men to herself, and to say that it is, as it were, the pendant and necklace of all of Greece, and a precinct of the Nymphs, since all the Naiads dwell here, and a chamber of the Seasons where they forever sit and from which they come forth when they have opened the gates — whether you wish to call them the gates of Zeus or Poseidon. But if the cities ever happened to contend about their beauty, as the goddesses are said once to have done among themselves, this city would have Aphrodite's role.

And what would one say about the appearance of the

city? Not even the eyes of all men are sufficient to take it in. 26. What more evidence would one offer of its greatness than that it has been extended to all the seas and has been settled beside and along them, not just the one but not the other, but all of them equally. 27. Indeed, the city was of old a starting point for good order, and even now administers justice for the Greeks. Indeed, you would see it everywhere full of wealth and an abundance of goods, as much as is likely, since the earth on every side and the sea on every side flood it with these, as if it dwelled in the midst of its goods and was washed all around by them, like a merchant ship.

28. While traveling about the city, you would find wisdom and you would learn and hear it from its inanimate objects. So numerous are the treasures of paintings all about it, wherever one would simply look, throughout the streets themselves and the porticos. And further the gymnasiums and schools are in themselves instruction and stories.

29. Why should I mention Sisyphus, or "Corinthus the son of Zeus," or Bellerophon the son of Poseidon, or any of the other heroes and demigods? Or again those who afterwards invented weights, scales, measures, and the justice inherent in these, and the story of how this city built the first ship, not only the trireme, but even the Argo itself, I would say? Indeed, the leader of its expedition clearly put in and anchored the Argo here because he put out from here. Or again the deeds on land, the so-called wings of Pegasus, whether you will speak of him as a horse or as a bird, and he who first dared to ride him, the flying knight?

30. But these are old and fabulous stories. Indeed, as to all its deeds in peace and war, which are still even now remembered, are they not more glorious than those of any Greek city, are they not more notable than any other's on land and sea? Whose deeds and actions are more distinguished?

31. But the present is not a time of war, so that it is not appropriate to raise the memory of such things when the

Greeks are celebrating a national festival and act in con-
cord in this the best and most famous national festival
—which assembles every two years and meets twice as
often as the others and draws up, surpasses, and again
overtakes the rest, just as in a chariot race, if it were
somehow possible for those who are mere human beings
to witness the course of Poseidon's chariot — and when
men assemble at the common wine bowl, and at the same
time make libations and sacrifices and launch the festival
pilgrimages for Poseidon, Amphitrite, Palaemon, and
Leucothea. Now it would be well for us to hymn these
things and to discuss them and speak about them.

This translation, by Charles A. Behr, admirably captures
the studied and affected phrasing which is characteristic of
Aristides' elliptical style; his concern to imitate Demos-
thenes comes across as a striving for effect which does
nothing to enhance the clarity of his message. The above
citation concerning Corinth is taken from an oration in
praise of Poseidon pronounced on the occasion of the Isthmian games (nn. 23 and 31). The other great panhellenic
festivals at Olymphia, Nemea, and Delphi were celebrated
every four years, and the bond of unity that Aristides highlights (n. 31) was a very old theme (cf. p. 15 above).

The use of 'here' throughout the oration indicates that
Aristides was in Isthmia, but the abundance of fine phrases
actually tells us very little about Corinth, and nothing that is
not known from earlier sources. The vague generalities
betray the lack of precise information. It was the capital of
the province of Achaia (n. 27), a city that grew rich on the
commerce facilitated by its advantageous geographical
location, "a kind of route or passage for all mankind" (n.
24). It was above all "a market-place" (n. 23) or "a merchant
ship" (n. 27), and entertained trade relations with a great
number of other cities (n. 24). The same commonplaces are
mirrored in his reference to the buildings (n. 28).

His talent for the generic phrase again appears in his
evocation of the mythological associations of Corinth (n.
29), which are explained by Pausanias (cf. above). He seems

to have been unaware of why Corinth was considered the city of Aphrodite (n. 25). Certainly, no other ancient author would have thought of this tough, driving commercial center (cf. Strabo, p. 58 above) as projecting an image of "beauty, desire, love, and friendly converse" (n. 25).

It is not difficult to imagine what Paul's reaction would have been if someone had informed him that there was no other place "where one would rest as on a mother's lap with more pleasure or enjoyment" (n. 24)! For all his praise Aristides knew very little about Corinth.

APULEIUS

Born in A.D. 123 at Madauros in north Africa, he was educated at Carthage and Athens. He travelled widely before settling down at Carthage (c. A.D. 161) where he was appointed chief priest after acquiring a reputation as a philosopher, poet and rhetorician. It is not known when he died. He is celebrated for his *Metamorphoses* (better known as *The Golden Ass*), the sole Latin novel to have survived intact. In a story which begins and ends at Corinth, he offers a lower-class view of Greek provincial society, which has been brilliantly synthesized by Millar (1981); this was the real world in which Paul moved.

METAMORPHOSES, 2:12

> I knew among us at Corinth a certain man of Assyria, who by his answers set the whole city in a turmoil, and for the gain of money would tell every man his fortune; to some he would tell the days they should marry; to others he would tell when they should build, so that their edifices should continue; to others where they should best go about their affairs; to others when they should travel by land; to others when they should go by sea.

The presence of a Chaldaean fortune-teller underlines the cosmopolitan character of Corinth, just as the questions he was asked emphasize its strongly commercial orientation.

METAMORPHOSES, 10:18

> But first I will tell you (which I should have done before) who my master was, and of what country. His name was Thiasus; he was born at Corinth, which is the capital of the whole province of Achaia. He had passed all offices of honor in due course according as his birth and dignity required, and he should now take upon him the office of quinquennial magistrate. Now to show his worthiness to enter upon that office, and to purchase the benevolence of every person, he appointed and promised public joys and triumphs of gladiators, to endure the space of three days. To bring his endeavor for the public favor to pass, he came into Thessaly to buy magnificent wild beasts and valiant gladiators for the purpose. . . . After a long time, when we had travelled as well by sea as land, and fortuned to arrive at Corinth, the people of the city came out to greet us.

The novel got its popular title, *The Golden Ass,* because the story is told by Lucius, a young man who has been turned into a donkey. At this point in the narrative, his master is a member of the upper class which effectively controlled Corinth. This is the only text to say that this city was the capital *(caput)* of Achaia. The city was ruled by two magistrates elected annually *(Duoviri)*. Every fifth year they had the additional duties of taking the census and of revising the membership of the city council (Wiseman, 1979:499). Only the wealthy could aspire to such office, because they had to be willing and able to make a significant financial contribution to the city (cf. pp. 14-15 above). A gladiatorial show (mentioned also by Dio Chrysostom, p. 95 above) was of less permanent value than public works done "in return for" office, e.g. a pavement (p. 37 above) or fifty housing units (Kent: n. 306).

Thessaly is a great plain surrounded by mountains in east central Greece. In summer it is one of the hottest places in Europe. The mountains still contain bears, wolves, and wild boar, all of which are mentioned by Apuleius (4:13; 7:22-24; 8:4, 15). Paul passed through this area on his journeys between Thessalonica and Corinth (1 Cor 16:5; 2 Cor 1:16). The exhaustion of crossing the plain in the heat no doubt increased his apprehension of being attacked by animals in the mountain passes.

METAMORPHOSES, 10:35

> I ran away with all my force, and came after about six miles very swiftly passed to Cenchreae, which is a most noble town of the colony of the Corinthians, bordering on the seas called Aegean and Saronic. There is a great and mighty haven frequented by the ships of many a sundry nation.

On Cenchreae, the eastern port of Corinth, see above p. 19. There Lucius had a vision of the goddess Isis (11:4), who informed him where to find roses to eat (11:6). Once he had done so, he recovered his human form (11:13) and joined the procession to the Temple of Isis (11:17), in whose vicinity he lived (11:19) until he became an initiate of the mystery (11:22-25).

ALCIPHRON

Alciphron was so insignificant a figure that he is not mentioned by any ancient author. His writings suggest that he borrowed from Lucian (c. A.D. 120-180) and from the Greek comedies of the 4th cent. B.C. Thus he must be placed towards the end of the 2nd cent. A.D. at the earliest.

LETTERS OF PARASITES, n. 24 (3:60)

Stuff-Cheek to Sleep-at-Table

I did not enter Corinth after all; for I learned in a short time the sordidness of the rich there and the misery of the poor. For example, at midday, after most people had bathed, I saw some pleasant-spoken, clever young fellows moving about, not near the dwellings but near the Craneum, and particularly where the women who peddle bread and retail fruit are accustomed to do their business. There the young fellows would stoop to the ground, and one would pick up lupine pods, another would examine the nutshells to make sure that none of the edible part was left anywhere and had escaped notice, another would scrape with his fingernails the pomegranate rinds (which we in Attica are accustomed to call *sidia*) to see whether he could glean any of the seeds anywhere, while others would actually gather and greedily devour the pieces that fell from the loaves of bread — pieces that had by that time been trodden under many feet.

Such is the gateway to the Peloponnese, the town that lies betwixt two seas, a town charming indeed to look upon and abounding in luxuries, but inhabited by people ungracious and unblessed by Aphrodite. And yet they say that, when Aphrodite rose from Cythera, she came to pay her respects to Acrocorinth; but possibly the women have Aphrodite, Guardian of the City, as their cult goddess, the men have Famine.

The point of this artistic little piece is clear; parasites will find few pickings at Corinth. Craneum, the most desirable suburb in the city (cf. p. 22 above), symbolizes the rich, just as the poor are concretized in the clever, smooth-tongued young idlers who have failed to attach themselves to a wealthy patron. For all its riches, Corinth had no welcome save for those who wanted to work. The image evoked is that of English industrial towns of the mid-19th century whose magnates were notoriously tight-fisted save as regards their personal comfort, and everyone was expected to earn what they needed.

The truth of this picture should not be accepted too easily for it is rooted in Athenian envy. In a previous letter another parasite writes to a friend, "I am hastening back from Corinth to Athens. . . . Surely it is better to lie outstretched, a corpse, before the Dioneïd Gate or Gate of the Knights, without a burial mound, than to endure the opulence of the Peloponnese." (n. 15; 3:51). In this period Athens could no longer rival Corinth in commerce but relied on her glorious past to attract tourists and benefactions (Larsen: 475); as a lucky idler it could condescend to the hard-working.

For all that, what is said about Craneum confirms Pausanias (cf. p. 22 above). It was at some distance from the built-up part of Corinth, and the presence of hawkers indicates that others took their pleasure there. The consistency of this observation with what we know of pre-146 B.C. Corinth makes the point relevant to any reconstruction of the city in the time of Paul.

DIO CASSIUS

Born in Nicaea in Asia Minor c. A.D. 160, Cassius Dio Cocceianus came to Rome as a young man. A place in the Senate and a career as a lawyer prepared him for a series of high offices due to his friendship with several emperors. He shared the consulship with the emperor Alexander Severus in 229, after which he retired and probably died within four or five years. He is remembered for his 80-volume history of Rome from its legendary beginnings to A.D. 229. His principal sources were Polybius, Livy, and if not Tacitus himself certainly the annalistic tradition he preserved. Only Bks 36-54 (68-10 B.C.) have been preserved intact. However, Bks 1-21 were paraphrased in the 12th cent. A.D. by Zonaras, who had been private secretary to the Byzantine emperor Alexis I Comnenus, and Bks 51-80 were abridged by Xiphilinus, an 11th cent. monk of Constantinople.

ROMAN HISTORY, 21 (= Zonaras, 9:31)

Diaeus now gathered a larger force and undertook to give battle to them, but, as the Romans did not come out against them, he conceived a contempt for them and advanced into the valley lying between the camps. Mummius, seeing this, secretly sent horsemen to assail them on the flank. After these had attacked and thrown the enemy into confusion, he brought up the phalanx in front and caused considerable slaughter. Thereupon Diaeus killed himself in despair, and of the survivors of the battle the Corinthians were scattered over the country, while the rest fled to their homes. Hence the Corinthians within the wall, believing that all their citizens had been lost, abandoned the city and it was empty of men when Mummius took it.

After that he won over without trouble both that people and the rest of the Greeks. He now took possession of their arms, all the offerings that were consecrated in their temples, the statues, paintings, and whatever other ornaments they had; and as soon as his father and some other men were sent out to arrange terms for the vanquished, he caused the walls of some of the cities to be torn down and declared them all to be free and independent except the Corinthians.

As for Corinth, he sold the inhabitants, confiscated the land, and demolished the walls and all the buildings, out of fear that some states might again unite with it as the largest city. To prevent any of them from remaining concealed and any of the other Greeks from being sold as Corinthians he assembled all those present before disclosing his purpose, and after causing his soldiers to surround them in such a way as not to attract notice, he proclaimed the freedom of all except the Corinthians and the enslavement of these; then, instructing them all to lay hold on those standing beside them he was able to make an accurate distinction between them.

Thus was Corinth overthrown. The rest of the Greek world suffered momentarily from massacres and levies of money, but afterward came to enjoy such immunity and prosperity that they used to say that if they had not been captured promptly, they could not have been saved.

So this end simultaneously befell Carthage and Corinth, those ancient cities; but at a much later date they received colonies of Romans, became again flourishing, and regained their original position.

This account of the fall of Corinth in 146 B.C. adds a number of details to the narratives of Pausanias (p. 43 above) and Strabo (p. 65 above). The most important one is the note that Mummius, the Roman general, made a serious effort to round up the Corinthians who had not been taken in the city. The impression is given that he assembled all the prisoners-of-war taken in the entire campaign and then used the provincialism of the Greeks to winkle out the Corinthians. How successful he was cannot be determined, but it is unlikely that he caught everyone. The point is significant for any determination of the continuity of Greek presence in the pre-146 B.C. and the post-44 B.C. cities.

ROMAN HISTORY, 43:50.3-5

It was a source of pride to Caesar that he had restored Carthage and Corinth. To be sure there were many other cities in and outside of Italy which he had either rebuilt or founded anew; still other men had done as much. But in the case of Corinth and Carthage, those ancient, brilliant and distinguished cities which had been laid in ruins, he not only colonized them, in that he recognised them as colonies of the Romans, but also restored them in memory of their former inhabitants, in that he honored them with their ancient names; for he bore no grudge, on account of the hostility of those peoples, towards places that had never harmed the Romans.

This stress on the preeminence of Corinth and Carthage among the many colonies founded by Julius Caesar (cf. PW 4:526-533) echoes Plutarch (p. 109 above), and is perfectly justified in terms of their development in the 1st and 2nd cents. A.D. However, since the colonists were sent out only shortly before Caesar's death in 44 B.C. (cf. Appian, p. 117 above), it would appear that the pride attributed to him is as much a figment of the author's imagination as the reason he gives for their foundation (cf. Strabo, p. 67 above).

PHILOSTRATUS

Flavius Philostratus was born on the island of Lemnos about A.D. 170, and studied in Athens before going on to Rome where the wife of the emperor Septimius Severus (A.D. 193-211) commissioned him to write a life of Apollonius of Tyana, an ascetic wandering teacher with miraculous powers. Nothing reliable is known about the career of Apollonius, save that he was active in the second half of the 1st cent. A.D. The documentation that Philostratus is supposed to have had at his disposition no longer exists, if indeed it ever did; the authenticity of the letters attributed to Apollonius is questioned. It is unlikely, therefore, that Philostratus had any genuine information concerning 1st cent. Corinth in which he sets part of the ministry of Apollonius.

He makes Apollonius predict both the conception and failure of Nero's project to dig a canal through the Isthmus (4:24), but he in fact tells us nothing more than Suetonius does (p. 114 above). The second episode is a mildly erotic tale of a young man in the toils of a vampire (4:25), a legend embroidered on the reputation of Corinth as the city of love. Finally, there is an encounter with an individual named Bassus (4:26), who is identified in a letter of Apollonius as a president of the Isthmian games (*Epistles*, 36). For reasons that are entirely unclear Bassus is assigned to the year A.D. 61 in the list of the presidents of the games (Kent: 31).

LIFE OF APOLLONIUS OF TYANA, 5:19

> Demetrius said that he had fallen in with Musonius at the Isthmus where he was fettered and under orders to dig. He addressed to him such consolations as he could, but Musonius took his spade and stoutly dug it into the earth, and then looking up said, "You are distressed, Demetrius, to see me digging through the Isthmus for Greece, but if you saw me playing the harp like Nero, what would you feel then?"

Gaius Musonius Rufus (A.D. 30-101), a Stoic philosopher, was banished from Rome for suspected involvement in the conspiracy to overthrow the emperor Nero in A.D. 65. He was confined on the barren island of Gyaros in the Aegean but, when Nero began work on the canal through the Isthmus of Corinth in A.D. 67, he was transferred to one of the chain gangs laboring there. Nero had absolutely no musical ability. *See* Suetonius (pp. 110-111 above).

LIFE OF APOLLONIUS OF TYANA, 7:10

> Apollonius, however, without revealing his intention even to Damis, set sail (from Smyrna) in his company for Achaia, and having landed at Corinth and worshipped the Sun about midday, with his usual rites, embarked in the evening for Sicily and Italy. And falling in with a favourable wind and a good current that ran in his direction, he reached Dicaerachia on the fifth day.

Here we have a perfect illustration of the 'passing traveller' mentioned by Favorinus (p. 100 above). Apollonius is represented as embarking from Smyrna (modern Izmir) in western Asia Minor. With favourable winds the voyage to Cenchreae would have taken less than five days. To cross the Isthmus to the port of Lechaeum was only a matter of three hours walk (fig. 1), and there he boarded ship again for Dicaerachia which is Puteoli (modern Pozzuoli), a port 8 kms from Naples in a bay to the west; it was there that Paul also landed en route to Rome (Acts 28:13). Philostratus may well have taken this route himself when he voyaged from Athens to Rome; certainly a multitude of others did throughout the centuries (cf. pp. 76 and 83 above).

ATHENAEUS

Nothing is known about Athenaeus beyond the sparse facts that he was a native of Naucratis in Egypt, and that he was active in Rome at the end of the 2nd cent. and beginning of the 3rd cent. A.D. He is remembered only because of a work called *Deipnosophistae* which has been wittily translated as *The Gastronomers*; the guests at a banquet discourse at length about every topic under the sun. This device was chosen by Athenaeus to enable him to integrate a vast number of quotations from ancient authors with his own interpretations and comments. Many of the works cited no longer exist, and without the data that he supplies our knowledge of ancient literature would be immeasurably poorer.

DEIPNOSOPHISTAE, 13:573c-574c

Now I am going to recite for your benefit, Cynulcus, a kind of Ionian speech, "spinning it out far," as Aeschylus's Agamemnon would say, on the subject of prostitutes; I will begin with the beautiful city of Corinth, since you have referred with insults to my residence there as a sophist.

It is an ancient custom in Corinth, as Chamaeleon of Heracleia records in his book *On Pindar*, whenever the city prays to Aphrodite in matters of grave importance, to invite as many prostitutes as possible to join in their petitions, and these women add their supplications to the goddess and later are present at the sacrifices. When, accordingly, the Persian invaded Greece, as Theopompus records, likewise Timaeus in the seventh book, the Corinthian prostitutes entered the temple of Aphrodite and prayed for the salvation of the Greeks. Hence also, when the Corinthians dedicated in honour of the goddess the tablet which is preserved even to this day, recording separately the names of the prostitutes who had made supplication on that occasion and were later present at the sacrifices, Simonides composed the following epigram: "These women were dedicated to pray to Cypris, with Heaven's blessing, for the Greeks and their fair-fighting fellow-citizens. For the divine Aphrodite willed it not that the citadel of Greece should be betrayed into the hands of the Persian bowmen."

Even private citizens vow to the goddess that, if those things for which they make petition are fulfilled, they will even render courtesans to her.

Such, then, being the custom regarding the goddess, Xenophon of Corinth also, when he went forth to Olympia to take part in the contest, vowed that he would render courtesans to the goddess if he won the victory. And so Pindar at first wrote in Xenophon's honour the eulogy which begins with the words, "Thrice victorious at Olympia is the house which I praise"; and later he wrote also the round which was sung at the sacrificial feast, in which, at its very beginning, he has addressed the courtesans who joined in the sacrifice when Xenophon was present and offered it to Aphrodite. That is why he has said: "O Queen of Cyprus! Hither to thy sanctuary Xenophon hath brought a troupe of one hundred girls to browse, gladdened as he is by his vows now fulfilled." But the beginning of the lyric is as follows: "Young girls, who welcome many strangers with your hospitality, ministrants of Persuasion in rich Corinth — who on the altar send up in smoke the auburn tears of fresh frankincense the many times that ye fly in thought up to the Mother of the Loves, heavenly Aphrodite; upon you, my children, free from reproach, she hath bestowed the right to cull the fruit of soft beauty in your desired embraces. When Necessity requires it, all things are fair." And so, having begun in this way, Pindar continues: "And yet I wonder what the lords of the Isthmus will say of me, seeing that I have devised such a prelude as this to a glee with honeyed words, linking myself with common women." It is indeed plain that in addressing himself to these prostitutes the poet was anxious as to how the affair was going to appear in the eyes of the Corinthians. But having full confidence in his own integrity, as it would seem, he straightway adds: "We have taught how to test gold by a pure touchstone."

But that the prostitutes also celebrate their own festival of Aphrodite at Corinth is shown by Alexis in *The Girl in Love:* "The city celebrated a festival of Aphrodite for the prostitutes, but it is a different one from that held separately for freeborn women. On these days it is customary for the prostitutes to revel, and it is quite in the mode for them to get drunk here in our company."

The relevance of this text lies in the probable relationship of its sources to Strabo's assertion that at Corinth more than 1000 temple-prostitutes served Aphrodite (p. 56 above). However, in the note on this latter passage it was pointed out that sacred prostitution was unknown in Greece and that consequently Strabo must be in error. This position is contradicted by the statement of Athenaeus that "Even private citizens vow to the goddess that, if those things for which they make petitions are fulfilled, they will even render courtesans to her." (573e). Hence, the accuracy of his information must be tested.

His dates make it clear that Athenaeus could not have had personal knowledge of what went on in pre-146 B.C. Corinth. What he says, therefore, must be based on the ancient authors he quotes. This raises two questions. Does he cite them accurately, for they must have been scribbled as reading notes before being incorporated in his book? And does he understand them correctly?

Conzelmann (1967:256) has pointed out that Theopompus in fact speaks of 'women' and not of 'prostitutes', and that the epigram of Simonides, which is the basis of Athenaeus' statement, may not have been accurately reported. As it stands, the impression is given that the women were dedicated to the goddess. The correct version is found in Plutarch (p. 108 above) where it is clear that the reference is to their statues. Thus, we are left with the statements of Chamaeleon and Timaeus that the prostitutes of Corinth joined the other women of the city in prayer to Aphrodite in moments of great danger. There is no hint that prostitutes as such functioned in her temple.

Nor is Athenaeus' claim substantiated by what follows. What he knows of Xenophon of Corinth comes from the ode which Pindar (518-438 B.C.) wrote for the feast celebrating the victories of the former in the Olympic games. All that can be inferred from Pindar, however, is that as part of his celebration Xenophon brought 50 or 100 prostitutes to a party which began with sacrifice in the temple of Aphrodite. Nothing suggests that he subsequently presented them to a sacred whorehouse (Conzelmann, 1967:255). Here, then, while quoting exactly, Athenaeus has misunderstood his source, perhaps because of the legend created by Strabo.

PART 2
WHEN WAS PAUL IN CORINTH?

Introduction

Paul himself mentions but one event linking his career with general history, his escape from Damascus when it was controlled by Aretas IV, king of the Nabataeans (2 Cor 11:32-33). Since Aretas died between A.D. 38 and 40, and since Damascus remained in Roman hands at least until the death of the emperor Tiberius on 16 March A.D. 37, this event permits us to give an approximate absolute date for the visit of Paul to Jerusalem mentioned in Gal 1:18 (Murphy-O'Connor, 1982a: 74-78).

Luke provides other links with general history but only two concern us here. He dates Paul's arrival in Corinth by reference to the Edict of Claudius (Acts 18:2), and situates at least part of his ministry there within the term of office of the proconsul Gallio (Acts 18:12); this latter is considered by all to be the pivotal date of Pauline chronology. Since both of these dates concern Corinth, I thought it appropriate to bring together here the textual data which serve as the basis on which these dates are established.

THE EDICT OF CLAUDIUS

Luke opens his account of Paul's visit to Corinth with the words, "After this he left Athens and went to Corinth. And he found a Jew named Aquila, a native of Pontus, lately come from Italy with his wife Priscilla, because Claudius had commanded all the Jews to leave Rome" (Acts 18:1-2). One very important witness, the Codex Vaticanus, omits the name of the emperor Claudius (A.D. 41-54), but this is certainly due to a scribal accident, because the grammatical structure of the phrase demands a proper name. Luke clearly suggests that Paul's arrival in Corinth followed very quickly on that of Aquila and Priscilla whose presence in the city is explained by a decree of Claudius. The problem, then, is to date the action taken by Claudius against the Jews of Rome.

The Texts

The dating of the Edict of Claudius depends on three texts which are here given in chronological order:

SUETONIUS, *Claudius*, 25:

> He expelled from Rome the Jews constantly making disturbances at the instigation of Chrestus.

DIO CASSIUS, *History*, 60:6.6:

> As for the Jews, who had again increased so greatly by reason of their multitude that it would have been hard without raising a tumult to expel them from the city, he did not drive them out, but ordered them, while continuing their traditional mode of life, not to hold meetings.

OROSIUS, *History*, 7:6.15-16:

> Josephus refers to the expulsion of Jews by Claudius in his ninth year. But Suetonius touches me more in saying, "Claudius expelled from Rome the Jews constantly making disturbances at the instigation of Christus." It cannot

be determined whether he ordered only the Jews agitating against Christ to be restrained and suppressed, or whether he also wanted to expel Christians as being men of a related faith.

The Text of Orosius

Orosius is the only one of the three authors to mention an explicit date; the expulsion took place in the ninth year of Claudius. According to Roman custom the regnal years of an emperor were counted from the moment he assumed power. Since Claudius was acclaimed by the Praetorian Guard on 25 January A.D. 41, his ninth year would have run from 25 January A.D. 49 to 24 January A.D. 50. In consequence, a great many scholars date Paul's arrival in Corinth to A.D. 49, e.g., most recently, Jewett (39). This information, however, cannot be accorded full confidence.

Ordained in Spain at an early age, Paul Orosius fled his native land in A.D. 414 because of the Vandal invasion. He became a pupil of Saint Augustine at Hippo in North Africa, and completed the book from which the above quotation is taken in A.D. 418. Entitled *Historiae adversum paganos*, it was designed to refute the allegation that the fall of Rome to Alaric in A.D. 410 was due to Christianity.

His dependence on sources is formally indicated by his references to Josephus and Suetonius. There is nothing in the writings of the Jewish historian that corresponds to the information given here, and the hypothesis of a slip of the pen resulting in the attribution to Josephus of something found in another source (no longer extant) does little to enhance our confidence in Orosius. Suetonius, on the contrary, is quoted accurately, but the interpretation that Orosius gives is coloured by his presuppositions. He does highlight a valid doubt as to who precisely were expelled (cf. below), and he is certainly correct in identifying Chrestus with Christ. However, he is guilty of anachronism in saying that Christianity was 'a related faith', for in the middle of the 1st cent. A.D. it was still not adequately distinguished from Judaism (cf. Acts 18:12-17). Moreover, Suetonius says nothing about 'Jews agitating against Christ'; he evidently thought Chrestus had been present in Rome as a rabble-rouser. Orosius may be thought to make the obvious correction, but he does not do so in a way which would indicate that he had perceived the problem.

Such doubts regarding the reliability of Orosius are reinforced by the silence of Tacitus. His *Annals* are complete for A.D. 49, but there is not a single allusion to any action, taken or contemplated, against the Jews of Rome in that year.

Efforts have been made to rehabilitate Orosius by arguing that indirect evidence corroborates his dating of trouble in Rome between Christians and Jews to A.D. 49; the most recent attempt is that of Smallwood (1981: 211-213). These arguments need to be examined briefly.

The first line of argument is well articulated by Smallwood, "it is conceivable that the first of them [i.e. Christian missionaries] reached Rome as early as c. 40, but the second half of the decade is much more probable, since the expansion of the Church beyond the bounds of Palestine before c. 40 was on a small scale and St Paul's wide-reaching evangelistic campaign did not begin until the mid-40s" (1981: 211). The dissension in the Roman synagogues provoked by such missionaries is thus to be dated to the end of the decade.

This argument furnishes no solid data. We are given a perfectly reasonable assumption, namely that the trouble mentioned by Suetonius was caused by Christian propaganda, plus a highly dubious estimate of when Christianity reached Rome. No one can say exactly when this happened, but it must be kept in mind that a Christian community had been established in Damascus by A.D. 33 at the latest, and that churches had been founded in Cyprus, Phoenicia, and Antioch in that same decade. To qualify this expansion of Christianity beyond the borders of Palestine as small-scale is not justified by the evidence. What is certain is that, from the beginning, believers were inspired to carry their new faith abroad. Contacts between Jerusalem and Rome were neither unusual nor difficult, and it is entirely possible that the first missionaries appeared in Rome towards the end of the 30's.

The second argument invokes the so-called Nazareth Inscription, which I give here in the translation of B. Metzger:

Ordinance of Caesar

It is my pleasure that graves and tombs — whoever has made them as a pious service for ancestors or children or members of their house — that these remain unmolested in perpetuity. But if any person lay information that another either has destroyed them or has in any other way cast out the bodies which have been buried there, or with malicious deception has transferred them to other places, to the dishonor of those buried there, or has removed the headstones or other stones, in such a case I command that a trial be instituted, protecting the pious services of mortals, just as if they were concerned with the gods. For beyond all else it shall be obligatory to honor those who have been buried. Let no one remove them for any reason. If anyone does so, however, it is my will that he shall suffer capital punishment on the charge of tomb-robbery.

On the face of it this document has no relevance to our problem, but the association with Nazareth inevitably provoked speculation. "The obvious interpretation of an enactment threatening tomb-robbers with the unusually harsh penalty of death, published near the scene of the major part of Christ's ministry, is that its author had heard the anti-Christian version of the Resurrection, that the disciples stole Christ's body from the bomb and spread the false story that He had risen from the dead, and was determined to prevent other new and disruptive sects from originating in similar outrages." (Smallwood, 1981:213). A judgement on the merit of this interpretation can safely be left to common-sense. The connection made with the point at issue is even more tenuous; the inscription could have been set up at

Nazareth only after A.D. 44, and the emperor's informants could only have been Jews incensed by the presence of Christian missionaries.

The extremely hypothetical character of this argument would be obvious even if the provenance and date of the inscription were established. In point of fact, however, we do not know where the inscription was set up; it owes its name to the fact that it was sent to France in 1878 *from* Nazareth. Nor is its date any more certain. There is a consensus that it is not a forgery, but the dates proposed (on the basis of letter forms) range from the end of the 1st cent. B.C. to the 2nd cent. A.D. (Metzger: 236). Thus, it is impossible to identify the emperor, and there is no necessary link with Christianity.

In sum, therefore, the indirect evidence corroborating Orosius evaporates on critical examination.

The Texts of Suetonius and Dio Cassius

Suetonius' style of composition (cf. p. 109 above) does not permit any conclusion regarding the date of the disturbance. Fortunately, it is otherwise in the case of Dio Cassius; his reference occurs in the context of his discussion of events in the first year of the reign of Claudius, i.e. A.D. 41 (Millar, 1964:40).

The most obvious objection to equating the event alluded to by Dio Cassius with the Lucan edict of Claudius is the observation that the former denies what the latter affirms, namely, expulsion of Jews from Rome. However, before accepting this discrepancy as decisive the matter must be looked at a little more closely.

According to Dio Cassius, Claudius first thought of expelling the Jews from Rome, and only when this was seen to be impossible — they numbered about 50,000 (Lüdemann: 186) — did he forbid them to assemble. This scenario, however, is totally implausible. The Jews had been equally numerous when Tiberius expelled them from Rome in A.D. 19 (cf. Smallwood, 1981:202-208), and it would have been preferable from an administrative point of view to expel them again. Jews were accustomed to meet every Saturday to prayerfully study the Law, and the effect of the refusal of this right would have been to create a perpetual grievance that could not but lead to periodic eruptions, which is precisely what the emperor was trying to avoid. In other words, the measure reported by Dio Cassius would have exacerbated, rather than solved, the problem.

Why, then, did Dio Cassius write as he did? To answer this we must remember that he wrote in the first decades of the 3rd cent. A.D. and necessarily had to rely on sources. What exactly these were, we do not know, but they must have belonged to the same annalistic tradition that served Suetonius and Tacitus. Thus, there is the distinct possibility that Dio Cassius had to rely on inaccurate information, and of course, he may have misunderstood what he read.

Light begins to dawn when we compare Dio Cassius and Suetonius. I have translated the latter's text (cf. above) in such a way as to bring out its most natural interpretation, i.e. Claudius expelled only the trouble-makers among the Jews. However, it could be read in another way, namely, "Since the Jews constantly made disturbances at the instigation of Chrestus, he expelled them from Rome" (Loeb translation). This would mean that all Jews were expelled. Dio Cassius' text looks very like a conscious correction of this reading (Lüdemann: 187). He was not aware of any such punishment, and so substituted what he considered a lesser penalty. However, he did not know that, in opposition to the central organisation of Alexandria, the Roman community was divided into a number of distinct synagogues (Smallwood, 1981:138), and so thought of the punitive action as affecting the entire Jewish population of the city. In all probability it would have been directed only against a single synagogue, which would have been closed until there was a guarantee that there would be no further disturbances.

This, of course, does not at all square with what Suetonius says, for he speaks of expulsion and not of closure. However, there are two difficulties in his account which makes its details suspect. He names Chrestus as the chief agitator but, as all have recognized, this is a misunderstanding of the role of Christ, whose person was the subject of the dispute. In addition, it was not legally possible to simply expel Jews who were Roman citizens; such a measure could be applied only to those who had no right of residence (Smallwood, 1981:216).

If neither Suetonius nor Dio Cassius can be taken at face value, we cannot conclude that they are referring to two distinct events. It is preferable, according to the rules of normal literary criticism, to see them as partial accounts, confused and inaccurate, of the same episode. The historical kernel underlying both accounts can be reconstructed as follows: as the result of a disturbance in a Roman synagogue concerning Christ, Claudius expelled the missionaries who were not Roman citizens, and temporarily withdrew from that Jewish community the right of assembly (Lüdemann: 188). This eminently plausible response to a potentially explosive situation would be dated, on the basis of Dio Cassius, to A.D. 41.

The above reconciliation of the accounts of Suetonius and Dio Cassius is admittedly tenuous, but it is confirmed by Philo. The great Jewish philosopher from Alexandria completed his *Legatio ad Gaium* in A.D. 41 at Rome while waiting for an audience with Claudius (Smallwood, 1970:30, 151). In it we find the following passage:

> Augustus, therefore, knew that they had synagogues and met in them, especially on the Sabbath, when they receive public instruction in their national philosophy. He also knew that they collected sacred money from their 'first-fruits' and sent it up to Jerusalem by the hand of envoys who would offer the sacrifices. But despite this *he did not expel them from Rome* or deprive them of their Roman citizenship because they remembered their Jewish nationality also. He introduced no changes into their synagogues, *he did not prevent them from meeting* for the exposition of the Law, and he raised no objection to their offering of 'first-fruits.' (nn. 156-157).

The relevance of the two italicized phrases to the point at issue is immediately obvious, and they become highly significant when it is recognized that in no source is there any hint that Augustus even contemplated such measures. Their point becomes clear if we assume with Smallwood (1981:214) that in A.D. 41 Philo had heard rumors of such actions on the part of Claudius. The latter revered Augustus as the model Roman ruler, and by citing Augustus as a counter-precedent Philo was in fact making a protest to which the touchy emperor could not take exception.

In sum, therefore, a very high degree of probability can be accorded to the hypothesis that as the result of an imperial action in A.D. 41 some Jews were expelled from Rome.

It has been objected, however, that this conclusion conflicts with what is known of Claudius' attitude towards the Jews at the beginning of his reign. He restored to them all the privileges which had been abrogated by his predecessor Gaius (Caligula). The letter has been preserved by Josephus in his *Antiquities of the Jews:*

> Tiberius Claudius Caesar Augustus, Germanicus, high priest, tribune of the people, chosen consul the second time, ordains thus:
>
> Upon the petition of king Agrippa, and king Herod, who are persons very dear to me, that I would grant the same rights and privileges should be preserved to the Jews who are in all the Roman empire, which I have granted to those of Alexandria, I very willingly comply therewith; and this grant I make not only for the sake of the petitioners, but as judging those Jews for whom I have been petitioned worthy of such a favour, on account of their fidelity and friendship to the Romans. I think it also very just that no Grecian city should be deprived of such rights and privileges, since they were preserved to them under the great Augustus.
>
> It will, therefore, be fit to permit the Jews, who are in all the world under us, to keep their ancient customs without being hindered in so doing. But I charge them

> also to use this my kindness to them with moderation, and not to show contempt of the superstitious observances of other nations, but to keep their own laws only.
>
> And I will that this decree of mine be engraved on tablets by the magistrates of the cities and colonies, and municipalities, both within and without Italy, both kings and governors, by means of the ambassadors, and to have them exposed to the public for full thirty days, and in such a place that it may be plainly read from the ground. (19:287-291).

The tenor of this letter leaves no doubt about Claudius' positive attitude towards Jews throughout the empire; all their traditional rights are reaffirmed in the most explicit and public way possible. However, the third paragraph contains a warning which should not be overlooked, "I charge them also to use this my kindness to them with moderation." Claudius does not give them *carte-blanche*; there are limits to what he is prepared to tolerate. This point is made formally in a letter addressed by Claudius to the city of Alexandria on 10 November A.D. 41, which complements the fulsome letter restoring Jewish privileges preserved by Josephus in *Antiquities of the Jews*, 19:281-285. In the translation of C. K. Barrett (46) the most important paragraph reads as follows:

> . . . . Wherefore once again I conjure you that on the one hand the Alexandrians show themselves forbearing and kindly towards the Jews who for many years have dwelt in the same city, and dishonour none of the rites observed by them in the worship of their god, but allow them to observe their customs as in the time of the deified Augustus, which customs I also, after hearing both sides, have sanctioned; and on the other hand I explicitly order the Jews not to agitate for more privileges than they formerly possessed, and not in future to send out a separate embassy as if they lived in a separate city, a thing unprecedented, and not to force their way into gymnasiarchic or cosmetic games, while enjoying their own privileges and

sharing a great abundance of advantages in a city not their own, and not to bring in or admit Jews who come down the river from Syria or Egypt, a proceeding which will compel me to conceive serious suspicions; otherwise I will by all means take vengeance upon them as fomentors of what is a general plague infecting the whole world. . . .

This document makes it perfectly clear that, from the outset of his reign, Claudius was prepared to react vigorously against anything that could be interpreted as a threat to public order. In A.D. 41 had certain Jews (from whom Christians were not distinguished) at Rome been seen as agitators, the emperor would definitely have moved against them in the way suggested by Suetonius and Dio Cassius. This year, therefore, certainly enjoys greater probability as the date of the edict of Claudius than the alternative of A.D. 49, which is based exclusively on the unreliable testimony of Orosius.

The Date of Paul's Arrival in Corinth

We are now in a position to try and fix the beginning of Paul's ministry in Corinth. Luke gives the impression that he arrived more or less on the heels of Aquila and Priscilla, who had 'recently' come from Italy as a result of the edict of Claudius (Acts 18:1-2). Thus, Paul would have arrived not long after A.D. 41. Unfortunately, things cannot be as simple as this.

In the first place, Luke is much less precise than appears at first sight. The edict of Claudius, as we have just seen, concerned only a single synagogue in Rome, and Luke does not say that Aquila and Priscilla came from that city; they came *from Italy*. Moreover, the edict involved only banishment from the city, not exile from the country. We cannot assume that the expelled Jews immediately took to the boats. It is more reasonable to assume that they took up residence somewhere outside the city in order to see how the situation would develop. How long they might have stayed, no one can say. Nor can we determine with any exactitude what Luke might have meant by 'recently.'

Secondly, other factors known from Paul's letters and from Acts have to be accounted for. Paul probably left Damascus for Jerusalem in late A.D. 37 (Jewett: 30-33). His first missionary journey (Acts 13-14) is estimated to have taken two years (Jewett: 161), and his second missionary journey, which brought him to Corinth, would have taken four years (Jewett: 59-61), but more likely five, if we include the delays imposed by winter in the high country. It can be shown from Paul's letters that this journey, which Luke for theological reasons places after the Council of Jerusalem (Acts 15-18), actually took place before that meeting (Murphy-O'Connor, 1982a). Thus, Paul could not have reached Corinth before A.D. 45.

This calculation, however, has to be modified by another factor. Luke tells us that when Paul left Corinth, after 18 months in the city (Acts 18:11), he went straight to Jerusalem (Acts 18:18-22). This was the second visit that Paul himself mentions in Gal 2:1. There, however, he tells us explicitly that it was fourteen years after his first visit at the end of A.D. 37. Hence, Paul may have left Corinth sometime in A.D. 51 (cf. p. 155 below), in which case his arrival should be placed in A.D. 49, i.e. a year and a half earlier.

These factors oblige us to recognize that Luke's vagueness in Acts 18:1-2 covers an uncomfortably large time span. Paul could not have arrived in Corinth until eight years after the edict of Claudius . Unless we are prepared to ignore the chronological data that Paul himself gives us in his letters, we must question whether there was any real relationship between the edict and the move of Aquila and Priscilla to Corinth. He probably had no real information on such a minor point, and combined vague memories to produce a scenario which, on other grounds, cannot be factual. If this hypothesis is correct, Acts 18:1-2 is parallel to Lk 2:2, for in this latter passage Luke claims that the motive for the journey of the Holy Family from Nazareth to Bethlehem was the census of Quirinius. This census, however, took place in A.D. 6-7 (Schürer: 399-427), some ten years after the birth of Jesus in the last days of Herod the Great who died in 4 B.C.

THE PROCONSUL GALLIO

"When Gallio was proconsul of Achaia, the Jews made a united attack on Paul and brought him before the tribunal" (Acts 18:12). This assertion that Paul's ministry in Corinth overlapped, at least in part, with the term of office of the Roman governor Gallio is the lynch-pin of Pauline chronology. It is the one link between the Apostle's career and general history that is accepted by all scholars. Our only means of dating the presence of this official in Corinth is a badly broken inscription containing a letter of the emperor Claudius.

Four fragments, discovered during the French excavations at Delphi, were first joined and published by Emile Bourguet in 1905. In 1910 he found three more fragments belonging to the same inscription; these were published by A. Brassac in 1913. However, H. Pomtow's refusal to admit that the new fragments belonged to the same text meant that they were ignored in all subsequent discussions of the inscription (e.g. Barrett: 48). In 1967 A. Plassart succeeded in joining the two groups of fragments, and added two more. His official publication of the nine fragments appeared in 1970. Since a number of his readings have been questioned by J. H. Oliver, a discussion of the Greek text on which the following translation is based is given in an Appendix.

The Text of the Inscription

> Tiberius Claudius Caesar Augustus Germanicus, 12th year of tribunician power, acclaimed emperor for the 26th time, father of the country, sends greetings to [_____]. For long have I been well-disposed to the city of Delphi and solicitous for its prosperity, and I have always observed the cult of the Pythian Apollo. Now since it is said to be destitute of citizens, as my friend and proconsul L. Iunius Gallio recently reported to me, and desiring that Delphi should regain its former splendour, I command you (sing.) to invite well-born people also from

> other cities to come to Delphi as new inhabitants, and to accord them and their children all the privileges of the Delphians as being citizens on like and equal terms. For if some are transferred as colonists to these regions . . . .

This translation makes no distinction between words preserved and those restored by the editors; those interested can easily work it out from the data given in the Appendix. Our first task is to establish when this letter was written. Then we shall consider its purpose, and try to determine to whom it was addressed. Finally, we shall attempt to work out the date of Gallio's term of office.

The Date of the Letter

The letter was written after Claudius had been acclaimed emperor for the 26th time. Such acclamations were ritualized public applause that sanctioned a triumph of the emperor, e.g. the conclusion of a successful military campaign or a specially significant victory. Unfortunately, we have no text which dates the 26th acclamation precisely. The problem, then, is to delimit as tightly as possible the time-span within which it could have occurred.

The upper limit is fixed by the 27th acclamation which took place before 1 August 52. Frontinus (A.D. 30-104), speaking of two aqueducts begun by Gaius, says:

> These works Claudius completed on the most magnificent scale, and dedicated in the consulship of Sulla and Titianus, on the 1st of August in the year 803 after the founding of the City (*Aqueducts of Rome*, 1:13).

The dedicatory inscription on one of these aqueducts, the Aqua Claudia, reads in part (Brassac: 42):

> Tiberius Claudius son of Drusus Caesar Augustus Germanicus Pontifex Maximus, 12th year of tribunician power, consul for the 5th time, acclaimed emperor for the 27th time, father of the country . . . .

Tribunician power was accorded to an emperor at the moment of his accession to the purple, and for each year of his reign he added one unit. Since the first tribunician year of Claudius was 25 Jan. 41 to 24 Jan. 42, his 12th year was 25 Jan. 52 to 24 Jan. 53. Thus, the year mentioned by Frontinus must be wrong, because 803 A.U.C. = A.D. 50; that this is due to scribal error is confirmed by the names of the consuls, because Sulla and Titianus held office in A.D. 52.

The 27th acclamation, therefore, took place between 25 Jan. 52 and 1 Aug. 52. This period, however, can be narrowed significantly. Acclamations were related to military prowess, and normally no major campaigns were undertaken in winter; the battle season was from late March to early November. Thus, the 27th acclamation must be dated between April and July 52. In consequence, the 26th acclamation must have taken place in the same period or prior to November the previous year. This ambiguity remains despite the perfectly preserved inscription from Kys in Caria which reads (Brassac: 44):

> Tiberius Claudius Caesar Germanicus Emperor God Augustus, Pontifex Maximus, 12th year of tribunician power, consul for the 5th time, acclaimed emperor for the 26th time, father of the country.

While this establishes a correlation between the twelfth year and the twenty-sixth acclamation, it does not exclude the possibility that the acclamation had been accorded prior to the beginning of the 12th year. The latter changed automatically on 25 January whereas acclamations were arbitrary. It should be kept in mind that the reference to the twelfth year in the letter under discussion is a *restoration,* and cannot be used as an argument.

The lower limit is fixed by a series of inscriptions (whose texts are substantially identical with that on the Aqua Claudia save for changes in the numbers; Brassac: 43) which affirm that the 22nd, 23rd, and 24th acclamations took place in the 11th tribunician year of Claudius, i.e. 25 Jan. 51

to 24 Jan. 52. No inscription correlates the 25th acclamation with a tribunician year.

At this stage we are forced into speculation on probabilities concerning the relation of six acclamations (the 22nd to the 27th inclusive) with two time spans, namely, the battle seasons April to November 51 and April to July 52. Since we have no dates for the 25th and 26 acclamations we have to assign them to one period or the other. The possibilities are:

1. *April-November 51*   *April-July 52*
   22 23 24   25 26 27
2. *April-November 51*   *April-July 52*
   22 23 24 25   26 27
3. *April-November 51*   *April-July 52*
   22 23 24 25 26   27

The criterion for a decision between the three options can only be the assumption that the symbolic value of the acclamations would diminish in direct proportion to their frequency. On this basis, possibilities 1 and 3 appear less probable than possibility 2. In the first there are too many acclamations in 52, while in the third there are too many in 51, but in the second we get a much better balance, i.e. the acclamations average one every two months. The argument is tenuous but, given the present dearth of evidence, it is the only one possible, and this must be kept clearly in mind when assessing the value of the conclusion.

In the above hypothesis the 26th acclamation would have taken place after the first significant victory in the spring campaign of A.D. 52, i.e. in April at the earliest. Thus, the letter of Claudius was probably written in the late spring or very early summer of that year.

The Purpose and Recipients(s) of the Letter

The purpose of the letter is to deal with a social problem, the depopulation of Delphi. There is no justification for supposing that the city was empty, as in an evacuation which might have followed a plague. We have to do with a significant drop in the number of citizens, which is most probably to be accounted for by a change in the economic situation. Delphi was not a trade-center; it was located off the main routes and in very difficult terrain, particularly in winter. It was the sanctuary of the Pythian Apollo, the oldest and most venerated shrine of Greece, and any decrease in the numbers of pilgrims would have affected the revenues of the city.

Delphi had been in decline for well over a century by the time this letter was written. It had been pillaged many times, but more importantly its prestige had evaporated. It survived on the memories of a glorious past, but it was no longer a vital spiritual center. As fewer visitors came, more families, unable to procure a livelihood, would have drifted away, with the inevitable consequence that even fewer services were available for those who did come.

This vicious circle appears to have engendered a sense of hopelessness, for the council which ran the city did not take the initiative in seeking imperial aid. The formulation of the letter clearly indicates that they did not petition the emperor either directly, or indirectly through the good offices of Gallio. The fact that the reaction of Claudius is expressed in the form of a command hints at a certain apathy, if not reluctance, on the part of the Delphians. He is certainly not acceding to a request for more citizens.

If such deductions regarding the circumstances of the letter are correct, it seems more probable that the letter was addressed to Gallio's successor as proconsul of Achaia than to the council of Delphi. Given the conditions of the time, it is difficult to see how the Delphians could have complied with a command addressed to them. If the city proved unattractive to those who had grown up there, what inducement could be offered to attract others from more prosperous towns? If the Delphians had decided to ignore the problem, what guarantee was there that they would expend themselves in achieving the emperor's desire? On the assumption that Claudius intended his command to be effective, it would have been more realistic to have confided the responsibility for its execution to his own governor, who had much wider powers of persuasion than any city council.

One possible objection to this conclusion derives from the fact that Achaia was a senatorial province (cf. Suetonius, p. 116 above). Hence, it might be argued, any communication to the proconsul would have to come from the senate, not the emperor, though the latter might address himself to an individual city. In theory, this is correct, but Roman practice in no way conformed to the theoretical distinction between types of provinces; for details, cf. p. 73 above.

The Date of Gallio's Term of Office

The view that provincial office-holders began their functions in 1 July is a deduction from an ordinance made in A.D. 15 by Tiberius that they "should take their departure [from Rome] by the first day of June" (Dio Cassius, 57:14.5). It is reasonable that adequate time was alotted for the journey. The departure date was advanced by Claudius in A.D. 42:

> The governors who were chosen by lot were to set out before the first day of April, for they had been in the habit of tarrying a long time in the city (Dio Cassius, 60:11.6).

Since this had little effect, presumably because travel conditions were still difficult in the early spring, he had to repeat the ordinance in a slightly mitigated form the following year, insisting that governors had to be out of the city by mid-April at the latest (Dio Cassius, 60:17.3). This has led some to think that the year of office began on 1 June. The purpose of the regulation was to ensure that governors got to their destinations in time, no matter how slowly they travelled.

Assuming that the average journey to a post would have taken a month, this would have given the newcomer a further month in which to familiarize himself with the local situation before assuming full responsibility. Some such arrangement was imperative because proconsuls held office for only one year, and one could not have a significant period of each year wasted while the new appointee found his way around.

We can safely assume, therefore, that a proconsul's term of office ran from the beginning of July to the end of the following June.

Since the letter of Claudius in which Gallio is mentioned was probably written in April or May A.D. 52, the last year in which Gallio could possibly have been proconsul is 1 July 51 to 30 June 52. However, we cannot argue that this was in fact the year from the title given to Gallio in the letter. Even if he were already out of office, he would naturally have been given the title which authorized his report to the emperor.

It is considerably more difficult to determine the earliest year that Gallio could have been proconsul. It does seem very unlikely, however, that he could have been appointed before A.D. 49. Only in that year did his brother, the philosopher Seneca, return from Corsica, whither he had been exiled by Claudius in A.D. 41. In the Roman system the disgrace of one member touched the whole family. Since Gallio does not appear to have been a man of exceptional character or ability, it is very probable that his nomination as proconsul of Achaia was materially assisted by the influence of his brother, who had been named to the imperial court as the tutor of Nero.

Theoretically, it is not impossible that Gallio served the two years, 50-52, because he may have been *extra sortem* (cf. p. 74 above), and officials of this type, like legates in the imperial provinces, served at the emperor's pleasure; their tenure was not limited to one year.

In reality, however, the question of Gallio's precise status is irrelevant because he did not complete his term of office. Thus, he only served part of 50-51 or of 51-52. We know this from a note by his brother Seneca:

> When, in Achaia, he began to feel feverish, he immediately took ship, claiming that it was not a malady of the body but of the place. (*Letters*, 104:1).

The impression of a fussy hypochondriac is confirmed by Pliny's report (*NH*, 31:62) that he felt the need for a long sea-voyage to recuperate after his consulship. If we accept what Seneca says of a 'malady of the place', it is natural to assume that Gallio took a dislike to Achaia and used a minor illness as an excuse to leave his post. Such an unreasoning aversion to a place is normally the result of a first impression; it may intensify with the passage of time, but it does not usually begin late. If this assessment is correct, it is unlikely that Gallio remained in Achaia more than five months, i.e. from June to the end of October.

Otherwise, he would have been stuck there for the winter. The danger of winter travel in the eastern Mediterranean is underlined by Luke, "The voyage was already dangerous because the Fast (i.e. Yom Kippur, celebrated near the autumnal equinox) was already over" (Acts 27:9; cf. 28:11). Pliny makes the same point more succinctly, "Spring opens the sea to voyagers" (*NH,* 2:47). The note of Dio Cassius, "If anyone ever risked a voyage at that season [winter] he was sure to meet with disaster" (60:11.2), is unconsciously confirmed by Suetonius who, after recounting how Claudius had been mobbed by the Roman crowd because of the lack of grain, continues, "After this experience he resorted to every possible means to bring grain to Rome, even in the winter season" (*Claudius,* 18). In other words, ships put to sea from November to March only for the most serious reasons, because one could be tossed by storms for three continuous months (Josephus, *Jewish War,* 2:200-203). In this season no one made a trip that could be deferred.

Even if Gallio did not depart before the winter, the *mare clausum* 'closed sea' has obvious implications for the time of the transmission of his report concerning Delphi to Rome. It was not a matter of high priority, and since we have no reports of any serious disturbances in Achaia in A.D. 50-52 which would demand immediate communication with the capital, it must be assumed that it went with the normal courier traffic outside the winter season.

Nothing so far has permitted us to choose between 50-51 and 51-52 as the year of Gallio's proconsulship. The only basis on which a decision can be made is Claudius' administrative ability. Did he deal with problems quickly or did he let them drag on? As usual, it is difficult to answer this question with any certitude. His life, as recounted by Suetonius, produces a very mixed impression. Claudius appears as extremely erratic:

> He showed strange inconsistency of temper, for he was now careful and shrewd, sometimes hasty and inconsiderate, occasionally silly and like a crazy man. (*Claudius*, 15).

This is certainly true if one looks at the emperor's life as a whole. A strict chronological order, however, imposes a different assessment. According to the *Oxford Classical Dictionary* (1949) two periods must be distinguished. From the period A.D. 41-50 "a large number of imperial enactments [survive and show]...profound administrative common-sense", but in the last four years his powers began to fail (p. 197). Just at the point that interests us, the weak side of his character began to predominate and we have no way of knowing how quickly he disposed of business. However, one factor disposes me to think that he reacted quickly to Gallio's information, namely, his known fondness for Achaia. According to Suetonius,

> He gave no less attention to Greek studies, taking every occasion to declare his regard for that language and its superiority ... and in commending Achaia to the senators he declared that it was a province dear to him through the association of kindred studies. (*Claudius*, 42).

It would be a mistake to imagine that Gallio had any particular interest in Delphi, or that his report was motivated by a high sense of duty. Delphi was the traditional center of the culture that the emperor admired so extravagantly, and Gallio was astute enough to recognize that evidence of his concern for that city would place him in the good graces of Claudius. Perhaps he even brought the report with him in an effort to assuage the imperial anger at his abandonment of his post. Be that as it may, it seems probable that Claudius would have reacted rather quickly to anything concerning Delphi. In this case, Gallio's report would have reached him at the earliest by late autumn A.D. 51 or at the latest when the sea was again opened for normal shipping in the spring of A.D. 52. Gallio's term of office, therefore, is more likely to have been A.D. 51-52 than the previous year.

The line of argument developed to support this conclusion is admittedly tenuous, but some such approach is necessary in order to justify the current consensus. It should also be noted that this consensus is no more than a lucky accident, because it depends on a misunderstanding of what the letter of Claudius was all about since only four of the nine fragments were used to reconstitute it (e.g. Haenchen: 66).

In the light of Seneca's statement that his brother did not finish his term of office, it is impossible to place Gallio's encounter with Paul (Acts 18:12-17) in the latter part of the proconsular year A.D. 51-52. The encounter must have taken place between July and October A.D. 51. Luke gives the impression that Paul left Corinth for Jerusalem shortly afterwards (Acts 18:18-22), but we cannot be sure that this corresponds to the reality; the juxtaposition of the two episodes may simply be a coincidence of Luke's method of composition. However, some confirmation that Luke may have reported the facts accurately is provided by the correlation of the dates of Paul's two visits to Jerusalem (cf. p. 148 above).

The Career of Gallio

Annaeus Novatus was born in the last decade of the 1st cent. B.C. as the eldest son of Lucius (or perhaps Marcus Annaeus) Seneca. He had two younger brothers, Lucius Annaeus Seneca, the philosopher, and M. Annaeus Mela. The family was rich and distinguished, but Annaeus Novatus was adopted by his father's friend, the senator Lucius Iunius Gallio, by whose name he was subsequently known.

Our information on his career is extremely patchy. His brother's remark that "he conquered honours by industry" (*Dialogues*, 12:7) must mean that he early entered public life. His advancement would have been interrupted by Seneca's exile (A.D. 41-49), but the latter's return to the center of power probably contributed to his appointment as proconsul of Achaia (1 July 51-30 June 52). This may have redeemed Claudius in his eyes, but Gallio's failure to complete his term of office (cf. above) probably drew on him again the imperial displeasure. His bile is manifested by a venomous witticism:

> Inasmuch as the public executioners were accustomed to drag the bodies of those executed in the prison to the Forum with large hooks, and from there hauled them to the river, Gallio remarked that Claudius had been raised to heaven with a hook. (Dio Cassius, 60:35.4).

This may have been designed to please Nero, to whom is attributed a remark in precisely the same vein. Claudius had been assassinated by being fed poisoned mushrooms (Dio Cassius, 60:34.2) and, when someone remarked that mushrooms were the food of the gods, the emperor, who was responsible for the murder, cynically agreed saying that "Claudius by means of a mushroom had become a god" (Dio Cassius, 60:35.4)

In any case, Gallio was soon in the good graces of Nero. His failure in Achaia forgotten, he was named consul in A.D. 58 (PW, 1:2237). The only evidence for his consulship is Pliny (*NH*, 31:62), and his name does not appear in the list of consuls. Consequently, he seems to have been no more than a stand-in, one of the *consules suffecti*. What he might have achieved has left no trace.

After the murder of his mother in A.D. 59, Nero felt free to indulge his art in public, and from his role as barker in the imperial circus Gallio must by then have become one of his intimates:

> As a fitting climax to these performances, Nero himself

made his appearance in the theatre, being announced in his own name by Gallio. (Dio Cassius, 61:20.1).

He is not mentioned among the conspirators who plotted the overthrow of Nero in A.D. 65. Seneca, however, was one of the leaders and, when the plan was revealed, he was permitted to die by his own hand (Dio Cassius, 62:24-25). The extent of Gallio's craven panic that his blood might implicate him is well brought out by Tacitus:

> In the senate, while all the members, especially those with most to mourn, were stooping to sycophancy, Iunius Gallio, terrified by the death of his brother Seneca and begging for his own safety, was attacked by Salienus Clemens, who styled him the enemy and parricide of his country. (*Annals*, 15:73).

The terror that Nero's irrationality inspired is easily imagined, and, if Gallio was singled out, his display of emotion must have been particularly grotesque. He is reputed to have died by forced suicide a year later (Suetonius, 96 R).

In the early 60's Seneca paid tribute to Gallio calling him "the most lovable of men, knowing no vice and hating all adulation ... the sweetest of all mortals" (*Natural Questions*, 4:10). The judgement does more credit to the author's charity than to his intelligence.

PART 3
ARCHAEOLOGY

Introduction

In previous sections mention has been made of aspects of Corinth which throw light on parts of Paul's correspondence with the Corinthians. Here I want to draw attention to four points where the contribution of archaeology is particularly significant. All concern buildings. The first three deal with the influence of the dimensions and emplacement of houses, temples, and shops, because these were factors which exercised considerable influence on the formation of house-churches, on the problems arising from meals in pagan temples, and on the way in which Paul exercised his apostolate. The fourth building is less important but it offers an amusing illustration of one passage in 2 Cor.

House-Churches and the Eucharist

Private houses were the first centers of church life. Christianity in the 1st cent. A.D., and for long afterwards, did not have the status of a recognized religion, so there was no question of a public meeting-place, such as the Jewish synagogue. Hence, use had to be made of the only facilities available, namely, the dwellings of families that had become Christian.

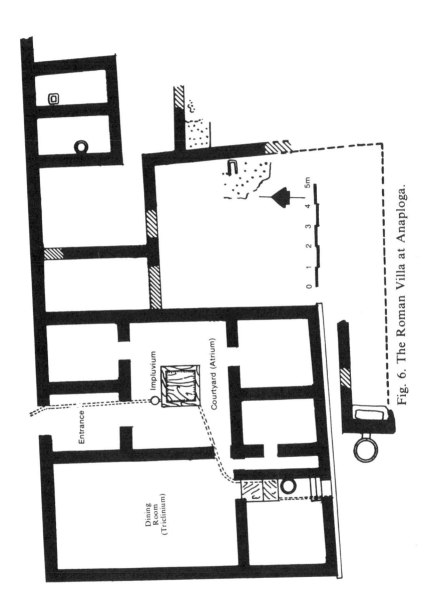

Fig. 6. The Roman Villa at Anaploga.

Four houses of the Roman period have been brought to light at Corinth (Wiseman, 1979:528). Of these only one can be attributed to the time of Paul, the villa at Anaploga (fig. 6); its location is shown in fig. 4. The magnificent mosaic floor of the triclinium (dining-room) is dated to the late 1st cent. A.D., and broken pottery in the fill laid to provide a level bed comes from the period A.D. 50-75, but the building was already in existence when the mosaic was created (cf. Miller).

Given the social conditions of the time, it can be assumed that any gathering which involved more than very intimate friends of the family would be limited to the public part of the house, and our concern here is to try and determine how much space was available.

In the villa at Anaploga the triclinium measures 5.5 x 7.5 meters giving a floor area of 41.25 sq. meters. This volume, however, would have been diminished by the couches around the walls; there would have been space for nine to recline. The atrium located just outside measures 5 x 6 meters, but the floor area of 30 sq. meters must be reduced also because at least one-ninth of the floor was taken up by the impluvium. This was a pool to collect the water that came through a hole of corresponding size in the roof; this was called the compluvium and was designed to light the atrium.

These dimensions were very typical, as can be seen from a number of comparisons. "Another sumptuous villa of the 2nd century has been excavated in the vicinity of the old Sicyonian Gate." (Wiseman, 1979:528). The adjective used should be noted, together with the formulation which indicates that it also applies to the villa at Anaploga. The five magnificent mosaic floors were published by Shear (1925:391-397). No plan is given, but the dimensions of the rooms are provided: atrium, 7.15 x 7.15 = 51.12 sq. meters with a square impluvium in the center; triclinium off the atrium, 7.05 x 7.05 = 49.7 sq. meters. The excavator considers it probable that the mosaic floors were made before 146 B.C. and were simply incorporated when the villa was rebuilt in the 2nd cent. A.D. The equally well-to-do House of the Vettii at Pompeii (fig. 7), destroyed by the eruption of A.D. 79, was of similar size; the atrium was 7 x 6 = 42 sq. meters, and the triclinium 4 x 6.3 = 25.2 sq. meters. The consistency of such figures for upper-class houses can be seen from the dimensions of the 4th cent. B.C. Villa of Good Fortune at Olynthus (south-east of Thessalonica on the coast); the triclinium was 5.8 x 5 = 29 sq. meters, and the atrium with its impluvium 10 x 10 = 100 sq. meters (fig. 8).

If we average out the floor areas for the four houses, the average size of the atrium is 55 sq. meters and that of the triclinium 36 sq. meters. Not all this area, however, was usable. The effective space in the triclinium was limited by the couches around the walls; the rooms surveyed would not have accommodated more than nine, and this is the usual number (Smith: 28). The impluvium in the center of the atrium would not only have diminished the space by one-ninth, but would also have restricted movement; circulation was possible only around the outside of the square. Thus, the maximum number that the atrium could hold was 50, but this assumes that there were no decorative urns, etc. to take up space, and that everyone stayed in the one place; the true figure would probably be between 30 and 40.

Let us for a moment assume that this was the house of Gaius, a wealthy member of the Christian community at Corinth (Rom 16:23), and try to imagine the situation when he hosted "the whole church" (1 Cor 14:23). From Paul's letters we know the names of 14 male members of the Corinthian community (Theissen: 94-95). We must suppose that, like Aquila, all were married. This brings us to 28 persons, which is obviously the minimum figure. Neither Luke nor Paul intend to give a complete list; mentions of particular names were occasioned by specific circumstances. Moreover, we are told that the households of two members of the community, Crispus (Acts 18:8) and Stephanas (1 Cor 1:16; 16:15-16), were baptized with them. Thus, we have to add an indeterminate number of children, servants/slaves, and perhaps relations. It would be more

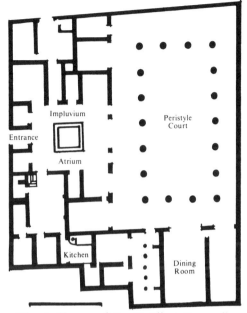

Fig. 7. House of the Vettii at Pompeii

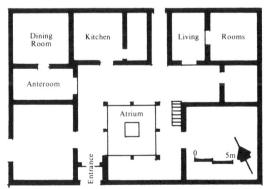

Fig. 8. Villa of Good Fortune at Olynthus

realistic, therefore, to think in terms of around 50 persons as a base figure.

This number could barely be accommodated in our average house of Gaius, but it would have meant extremely uncomfortable overcrowding in the villa at Anaploga. It would appear, therefore, that a meeting of "the whole church" (Rom 16:23; 1 Cor 14:23) was exceptional; it would simply have been too awkward. Moreover, as Banks (38) has pointed out, the adjective 'whole' is unnecessary if Corinthian Christians met only as a single group, and so must be understood to imply that other groups existed. This observation suggests that the formulae "the whole church" and "the church in the house of X" (Rom 16:5; 1 Cor 16:19; Col 4:15; Philem 2) should not be equated, but contrasted.

"The church in the house of X", then, would be a sub-group of the larger community. If Aquila and Priscilla/ Prisca acted as the center of such a sub-group in Ephesus (1 Cor 16:19) and Rome (Rom 16:5) it is very probable that they did likewise in Corinth. Such sub-groups would have been made up of the family, servants, and a few friends who lived in the vicinity (Banks: 38-39). While such sub-groups would have tended to foster an intimate family-type atmosphere, they would also have tended to promote divisions within the wider city community. It seems likely that the various groups mentioned by Paul in 1 Cor 1:12 would regularly have met separately. Such relative isolation would have meant that each group had a chance to develop its own theology, and virtually ensured that it took good root before being confronted by other opinions.

The difficulty of getting the whole church together regularly in one place goes a long way towards explaining the theological divisions within the Corinthian community, but the difficulties of the physical environment also generated other problems when all the believers assembled as a church.

The mere fact that all could not be accommodated in the triclinium meant that there had to be an overflow into the atrium. It became imperative for the host to divide his guests into two categories; the first-class believers were invited into the triclinium while the rest stayed outside. Even a slight knowledge of human nature indicates the criterion used. The host must have been a wealthy member of the community and so he invited into the triclinium his closest friends among the believers, who would have been of the same social class. The rest could take their places in the atrium, where conditions were greatly inferior. Those in the triclinium would have *reclined*, as was the custom (cf. 1 Cor 8:10) and as Jesus always did with his disciples (Jeremias: 48-49), whereas those in the atrium were forced to *sit* (1 Cor 14:30).

The space available made such discrimination unavoidable, but this would not diminish the resentment of those provided with second-class facilities. Here we see one possible source of the tensions that appear in Paul's account of the eucharistic liturgy at Corinth (1 Cor 11:17-34). However, his statement that "one is hungry while another is drunk" (v. 21) suggests that such tensions were probably exacerbated by another factor, namely, the type of food offered.

Since the Corinth that Paul knew had been refounded as a Roman colony in 44 B.C. and since Latin was the official language up to the end of the 1st cent. A.D., it is legitimate to assume that Roman customs enjoyed a certain vogue. One such custom was to serve different types of food to different categories of guests. Pliny the Younger recounts the following experience:

> I happened to be dining with a man, though no particular friend of his, whose elegant economy, as he called it, seemed to me a sort of stingy extravagance. The best dishes were set in front of himself and a select few, and cheap scraps of food before the rest of the company. He had even put the wine into tiny little flasks, divided into three categories, not with the idea of giving his guests the opportunity of choosing, but to make it impossible for them to refuse what they were given. One lot was intended for himself and for us, another for his lesser friends (all his friends are graded), and the third for his and our freedmen.... (*Letters*, 2:6)

The same custom naturally proved fair game for the Roman satirists of the 1st cent. A.D. The entire Fifth Satire of Juvenal is a vicious dissection of the sadism of the host who makes his inferior guests "prisoners of the great smells of his kitchen" (line 162). With much greater brevity Martial makes the same point with equal effectiveness:

> Since I am asked to dinner, no longer, as before a purchased guest, why is not the same dinner served to me as to you? You take oysters fattened in the Lucrine lake, I suck a mussel through a hole in the shell. You get mushrooms, I take hog funguses. You tackle turbot, but I brill. Golden with fat, a turtledove gorges you with its bloated rump, but there is set before me a magpie that has died in its cage. Why do I dine without you, Ponticus, though I dine with you? The dole has gone: let us have the benefit of that; let us eat the same fare. (*Epigrams*, 3:60).

> We drink from glass, you from murrine, Ponticus. Why? That a transparent cup may not betray your two wines. (*Epigrams*, 4:85)

Only the wealthy are attracted by this method of saving, and it is entirely possible that a Corinthian believer, responsible for hosting the whole church, found it expedient to both demonstrate his sophistication and exercise financial prudence by serving different types of food to the two groups of believers — a distinction imposed on him by the physical arrangement of his house. Since the host's friends were of the leisured class they could arrive early and feast on larger portions of superior food while awaiting the arrival of lower class believers who were not as free to dispose of their time. The condition of those reclining gorged in the triclinium could hardly be disguised from those who had to sit in the atrium.

The reconstruction is hypothetical, but no scenario has been suggested which so well explains the details of 1 Cor 11:17-34. The admonition "wait for one another" (v. 34) means that *prolambanô* in v. 21 necessarily has a temporal connotation; some began to eat before others. Since these possessed houses with plenty to eat and drink (vv. 22, 34), they came from the wealthy section of the community and might have made a contribution in kind to the community meal. This, they felt, gave them the right to think of it as 'theirs' (*to idion deiphon*). Reinforced by the Roman custom they would then have considered it their due to appropriate the best portions for themselves. Such selfishness would necessarily include a tendency to take just a little more, so that it might happen that nothing was left for the 'have-nots' (v. 22), who in their hunger had to content themselves with the bread and wine provided for the Eucharist. However, as Paul is at pains to point out, under such conditions no Eucharist is possible (v. 20).

Temple Banquets and the Body

A major portion of 1 Cor (chs. 8-10) is taken up with the question of the legitimacy of eating meat offered to idols. About the only time that meat came on the market was after pagan festivals and it had been part of the victims sacrificed to the gods. Some members of the Christian community (the Strong) argued correctly that eating such meat did not pose a moral problem, whereas for others (the Weak) it certainly did (Murphy-O'Connor, 1978). The situation could arise in private homes (1 Cor 10:27; cf. Plutarch, p. 104 above), but also in pagan temples. The Strong had no difficulty in participating in temple banquets, but this, according to Paul, generated an intolerable pressure on the Weak which forced them to violate their consciences, "If anyone sees you, a man of knowledge, reclining at table in an idol's temple might not the conscience of the weak person be 'edified' to eat food offered to idols? ... And so by your knowledge this weak person is destroyed, the brother for whom Christ died" (1 Cor 8:10-11). An examination of the Asclepion at Corinth reveals how easily this could happen.

The temple of Asclepius is located just inside the north wall (fig. 4) and is referred to by Pausanias (p. 37 above), who moreover notes that the site was a place of refreshment in summer. This, according to Vitruvius, should be the principal criterion in the location of a healing temple:

> For all temples there shall be chosen the most healthy sites with suitable springs in those places where shrines are to be set up, and especially for Asclepius and Salus, and generally for those gods by whose medical power sick persons are manifestly healed. For when sick persons are moved from a pestilent to a healthy place and the water supply is from wholesome fountains, they will more quickly recover. So will it happen that the divinity (from the nature of the site) will gain a greater and higher reputation and authority. (*On Architecture*, 1:2.7).

The pleasant cynicism of the last remark underlines the realism that went into the selection of the site. Obviously, the same qualities would have made the locality a place of relaxation, and this is confirmed by the presence of a large swimming pool a little way to the west (cf. Pausanias, p. 36 above). Like Craneum on the lower slopes of Acrocorinth on the other side of the city (cf. Pausanias, p. 22 above), it would have been one of the more pleasant quarters of the city.

Constructed in the 4th cent. B.C. (Wiseman, 1979:487), the sanctuary of Asclepius (fig. 9) was damaged when the city was sacked in 146 B.C. The temple proper was restored by the colonists of 44 B.C., but the colonnade around the fountain courtyard was not rebuilt (Wiseman, 1979:510, 512). Thus, it is not certain that the three dining rooms, built below the abaton on the east side of the courtyard (fig. 10), were actually functioning at the time of Paul. However, usage of the area cannot be excluded. Water was not so abundant that the spring and water collection tunnels could be casually abandoned. Even without the colonnade the open square in front of the dining rooms would have been a perfect little piazza, sheltered from the wind by the city wall and the surrounding buildings. In all probability it would have been frequented, not only by patients of the Asclepion,

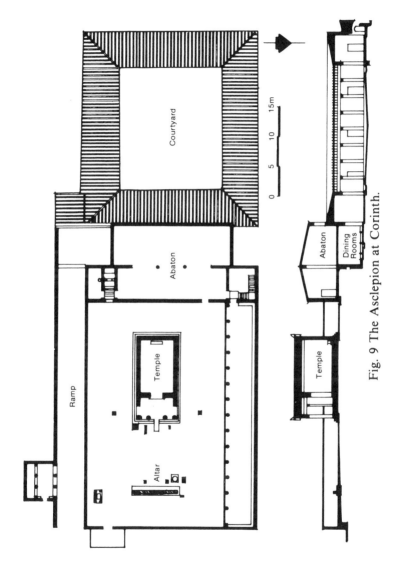

Fig. 9 The Asclepion at Corinth.

but also by casual visitors seeking a moment's respite from the noise and bustle of the city.

The disposition of each of the three dining rooms was the same. The couches around the walls could accommodate eleven persons. In front of them were seven small tables. The square slab in the center was cracked and blackened by fire, showing that cooking was done in the dining room. The facilities belonged to the temple but they could be used by private parties, who naturally would be expected to provide their own services. Some of the functions would have been purely social in character, but others would have been gestures of gratitude to the god for such happy events as a cure, a birth, a coming of age, or a marriage (Youtie: 14-15). The location of the dining rooms inevitably conferred a religious character on the parties held there, but very often this was explicitly underlined by the invitation, e.g.:

> Herais asks you to dine in the room of the Serapheion (= Asclepion) at a banquet of the Lord Seraphis tomorrow the 11th from the 9th hour. (*New Documents*: n. 52)

It is easy to perceive the dilemma that one of the Weak would face if he received such an invitation to celebrate the marriage of his pagan brother. He could not decline on the grounds that his new faith did not permit it, because the Strong were known to participate in such banquets. No matter how deeply rooted his conviction that Christians could not share in such meals there was no way he could make it either comprehensible or palatable to his family. To refuse could only appear as a gratuitous insult to a family he still loved. If he ceded to the legitimate desires of his family, he would be going against his conscience, and all because the Strong participated in such occasions.

Even if a formal invitation permitted the Weak time to concoct a good excuse, e.g. a business trip to Athens, there were other scenarios possible. Suppose one of the Weak was merely taking his ease in the court outside the dining rooms whose doors permitted outsiders to see and be seen. Suddenly a voice calls, "Come and join us!" He turns to see a group of the Strong ensconced on the couches, among whom may have been his employer or someone whom he could not afford to offend. Under such circumstances it would not always have been easy to find a reasonable excuse not to participate.

It is entirely probable that the wealthier members of Paul's flock had been wont to repair to the salubrious spot for recreation; it may well have been the closest the city got to a country-club with facilities for dining and swimming. It would have been natural to continue going there after conversion, because the commonsense estimate of the value of the site would have survived the demise of their belief in the god.

One of the features of the excavation of the Asclepion was the huge number of terracotta ex-votos representing heads, hands and feet, arms and legs, breasts and genitals, eyes and ears (Lang: 14). These represented the afflicted members cured by the god. It has been recently suggested that these contributed to the formation of Paul's concept of the Christian community as the Body (Hill), but with insufficient insight into Paul's theology to perceive the associative process.

The theme of the Body appears first in 1 Cor, and the way in which Paul formulates his remarks clearly indicates that it formed part of his oral preaching in Corinth. Furthermore, it is only in 1 Cor 12:12-31 that he mentions hands, feet, eyes, genitals, etc., as part of his effort to clarify the relation of believers to one another and to Christ. Sound methodology, therefore, demands that we look first to Corinth for the source of his inspiration. However, the ex-votos of the Asclepion could have functioned as Hill claims only because of another factor. From the beginning Paul had seen that love was fundamental to the Christian life (1 Thess 4:9). Hence, he must have been convinced that the community of the believers should be characterised above all by union. His problem was to find an image capable of conveying clearly to his hearers that the reality of Christian life went beyond mere coordination and cooperation; for him it was a question of shared existence, since the

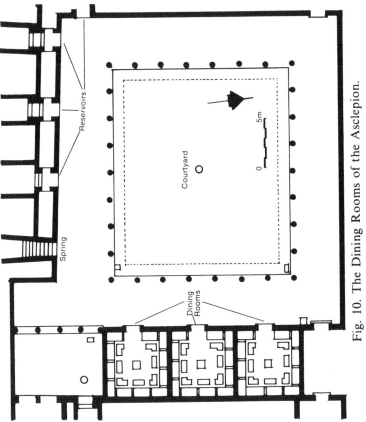

Fig. 10. The Dining Rooms of the Asclepion.

lover and the beloved are one. Against this background Paul would have seen the dismembered limbs displayed in the Asclepion as symbols of everything that Christians should *not* be: 'dead', divided, unloving and unloved. From this it would have been an easy step to the contrasting image of the whole body in which the distinctive identity of each of the members is rooted in a shared life. Since this is precisely what Paul wanted to see in the Christian community it would have been natural for him to conceive it in terms of a Body.

Even if Paul were aware of contemporary speculation on the body politic, some such trigger experience as the ex-votos of the Asclepion would have provided is necessary to explain the transfer of the Body concept to the church, because the structures of civil society were precisely the antithesis of what he was trying to achieve (Murphy-O'Connor, 1982b).

The Work Place and the Apostolate

There are two versions of Paul's arrival in Corinth. According to the Western text of Acts 18:3, "Paul was known to Aquila, because they were of the same tribe, and he remained with him." The Alexandrian text of the same verse is significantly different, "He came to them and, because they were of the same trade, he stayed with them and they worked, for they were tentmakers by trade." This is not the place to enter into a detailed discussion of the two versions; it can be argued that both are in fact the work of Luke.

There is no doubt that Paul supported himself by manual labour while ministering at Corinth. If he had done so both before (at Thessalonica; 1 Thess 2:9) and afterwards (at Ephesus; 1 Cor 4:12), it is eminently probable that he also worked in Corinth. This inference is made certain by the argument of 1 Cor 9:3-19; Paul could not have claimed to preach the gospel free of charge unless he had ensured his own livelihood.

Since Paul worked with his hands for the greater part of his life it is somewhat surprising to find that the language he

uses when referring to work clearly betrays a rather snob-
bish upper-class attitude towards manual labour; it was
slavish and demeaning (Hock: 1978). Why then did he
undertake it? Because he had little choice. Having chosen
the vocation of an itinerant preacher, the only options open
to him were to charge fees for his teaching, to beg, or to
work (Hock, 1980:52). The first two were unacceptable,
because they would diminish his credibility and restrict his
audience, and so only work remained.

At first sight the trade of tentmaker would appear particularly inappropriate for one whose ministry focused on
cities, but there was a tendency among artisans of the period
to use specialized titles, even when their work actually
covered a much broader range (Hock, 1980:21), much in the
same way as a carpenter of today will sometimes describe
himself as a cabinet-maker. Paul was in all probability a
leather-worker who could turn his hand to the production
of the wide variety of articles made of this material: thongs,
gourds for water and wine, harness, saddles, shields, etc.
Tents were also made from leather and a ready market
would have existed at Corinth. The great crowds of visitors
who came for the Isthmian games (p. 14 above) were housed
in tents, and the traders who flocked out from the city to
serve them needed portable booths. Tents were used by
travellers on merchant ships, and the crews sometimes
camped on shore when in port (Hock, 1980:34). In addition
to production, repair-work would have been an important
factor in the volume of business.

The excavation of Corinth has provided valuable clues to
the conditions in which Paul worked, and so adds a concrete
dimension to Hock's study (1979). A whole series of small
shops have been brought to light (fig. 5, nn. 7, 20, 29, 31, and
part of 35). The North Market (fig. 5, n. 8) had been completed not long before Paul arrived. It was a series of shops
around a central square, and their size is an adequate guide
to the dimensions elsewhere. They had a uniform height of 4
meters, and were just under 4 meters deep; the width varied
from 2.8 to 4 meters (De Waele: 439-441). Frequently they
had a communicating door or window with the shop
nextdoor.

The space was not as cramped as one might have expected, but it was diminished by the need to stock raw materials and to position worktables. The doorway was the only source of light, and this would have created problems in the cold of winter. The heat of a brazier would have been counteracted by the wind coming through the door, and working conditions would have been decidedly uncomfortable. It is not at all improbable that Paul wrote with such big letters (Gal 6:11) because he had to work barehanded in the cold (Deissmann: 49).

The way the participle and main verb are combined in 1 Thess 2:9, "working we proclaimed," indicate that Paul did not separate work and preaching. Indeed, one of the advantages of leather-working was that he could easily do both; the environment was clean and pleasant, and the only sound the soft thump as the awl went in. A good worker can get the needle and thread through the closing hole almost quicker than the eye can perceive and without apparently looking.

From a shop in a busy market or giving on to a crowded street Paul had access, not only to co-workers and clients, but also the throng outside. In slack periods he could stand in the door and button-hole those whom he thought might listen, a more efficient procedure than trying to gather a crowd in the agora (cf. Acts 17:17). It is difficult to imagine that his dynamic personality and utter conviction did not quickly make him a 'character' of the neighbourhood, and this would have drawn the curious, not merely the idlers but also those genuinely seeking.

The workshop also provided other advantages. Those attracted by his message could come in to question or chat as he worked. Married women with their attendants, who had heard of him, could visit on the pretext of coming to buy. In times of stress, when persecution or simple harassment threatened, believers could encounter him as clients. The workshop also brought him into contact with municipal officials. Did he meet Erastus (cf. p. 37 above) when paying rent or taxes?

In sum, therefore, the workshop was a very astute choice for a missionary center, but it should not be imagined that

Paul thereby had it easy. The average artisan of the period barely made ends meet (Hock, 1980:34), and in Paul's case his wandering life made it difficult for him to build up the local reputation that outweighs competition. Long hours of exhausting toil were necessarily his lot, and how many times did he have to start all over again in another small shop in a strange city?

Appendix

THE GREEK TEXT OF THE GALLIO INSCRIPTION

1 Τιβέρ[ιος Κλαύδιος Καῖσα]αρ Σ[εβαστ]ὸς Γ[ερμανικός, δημαρχικῆς ἐξου]

2 σίας[τὸ ΙΒ, αὐτοκράτωρ τ]ὸ ΚΣ, π[ατὴρ π]ατρί[δος - - - - χαίρειν].

3 Πάλ[αι μὲν τ]ῆι π[όλει τῇ] τῶν Δελφ[ῶν ἦν ο]ὑ μό[νον εὔνους ἀλλ' ἐπιμελὴς τῆς τύ]

4 χης, ἀεὶ δ'ἐτήρη[σα τὴ]ν θρησκεί[αν τ]οῦ Ἀπό[λλωνος τοῦ Πυθίου. ἐπεὶ δὲ]

5 νῦν λέγεται καὶ [πολ]ειτῶν ἔρη[μο]ς εἶναι, ὥ[ς μοι ἄρτι ἀπήγγειλε Λ. Ἰού]

6 νιος Γαλλίων ὁ φ[ίλος] μου κα[ὶ ἀνθύ]πατος, [βουλόμενος τοὺς Δελφοὺς]

7 ἔτι ἔξειν τὸν πρ[ότερον κόσμον ἐντελ]ῆ, ἐ[ντέλλομαι σε καὶ ἐξ ἄλ]

8 λων πόλεων καλ[εῖν εὖ γεγονότας εἰς Δελφοὺς ὡς νέους κατοίκους καὶ]

9 αὐτοῖς ἐπιτρέ[πειν ἐκγόνοις τε τὰ] πρεσ[βεῖα πάντα ἔχειν τὰ τῶν Δελ]

10 φῶν ὡς πολε[ίταις ἐπ'ἴσῃ καὶ ὁμοία. ε]ἰ μὲν γάρ τι[νες - - - ὡς πολεῖ]

11 ται μετωκίσ[αντο εἰς τούτους τοὺ]ς τόπους, κρ[

12 [το]ύτους [   ]ν πάντως ε[

13   ]σθη. οἵτινε[ς δὲ

14   ]ι καὶ τὸ συναύ[ξειν

15   ὥσπε]ρ ἐπὶ τῶν ἀνα[

16 ἀνα[φ]ημι < [Τ]οῖς μέντ[οι

17 εις τῶν[   ]είᾳ σε ἐντέλλομαι, ἵν[α

18 κατὰ προ[σῆκον πάντων] τῶν ἐν αὐτῷ γεγραμ[μένων μηδὲν] ἐριστὸ[ν ἦι]

This text is based on the nine fragments reassembled by Plassart, and is sensibly different from the traditional version (SIG. 3rd. ed., 2:801, reproduced in Hennequin: 358 and Jackson-Lake: 461), based on only four fragments, which served most of the introductions and commentaries still in use (e.g. Haenchen: 66).

Lines 1-2

Plassart and Oliver agree on omitting the title *archiereus megistos* which was restored in the traditional version; there is no space for it. The restoration of *to IB* is justified by the type of calculation developed on p. 143 above, and is confirmed by an inscription from Kys in Caria (text in Brassac: 44). According to Plassart, the name of the recipient(s) would have occupied 11 to 16 letter-spaces.

Lines 3-4

Here Plassart and Oliver differ on only one word; the former has *ephrontisa* where the latter has *epimelês*. The difference is not material.

Line 5

The restoration of this line is certain, since it is impossible to think of any other insertions that would make sense. The correct reading of two letters excludes the previous restoration, which was *nyn legetai kai* [*pol*]*eitôn eri*[*des e*]*keinai, ô*[*n mnêmên pepoiêtai Leukios Iou*]. In the interpretation of the letter no weight can be given to the adverb *arti*. The number of letters is necessary to make up the line-length, but the same result can also be achieved by writing out the praenomen in full.

Line 6

Since Gallio's name and title appear in the nominative case, he cannot be the recipient of the letter.

Line 7

The second restoration is the first serious divergence between Plassart and Oliver; where the former has *se* the latter has *hymein*. The reason is their differing views of line 17, where the problem will be discussed.

Line 8

The restoration of the end of the previous line and the beginning of this one, *ex al*[*lôn poleôn kal*]*ein*, is certain. Such being the case, one would expect the letter to specify who were to be invited and what inducements were to be offered in order to attract them. From this point of view

Oliver's restoration is certainly preferable to that of Plassart. Not only does he succeed in filling the line, but he underlines the obvious by restoring *eu gegonotas*; it would have been out of the question for Delphi to accept settlers of the servile class.

Line 9

Plassart leaves a gap of 12 letters, which Oliver fills with *ekgonois te ta*. Grants of citizenship necessarily included the future offspring of the settlers.

Line 10

There is no hesitation in restoring *hôs pole*[*itais*. Plassart continues with *gegonosin. Hoso*]*i*, but this stops uncomfortably short; one would expect an adjectival modifier. Moreover, *hôs poleitais gegonosin* adds nothing to *ta presbeia panta ta tôn Delphôn* (line 9); it is in fact completely tautological. These difficulties are satisfactorily dealt with by Oliver, who restores *hôs pole*[*itais ep' isêi kai homoiai*, namely *dikêi*. Not only is this the usual formula in a grant of citizenship, but it is precisely the sort of modifier one would expect. The *hôs* now makes perfect sense, because the phrase it introduces reinforces *panta ta presbeia*. Neither Plassart nor Oliver completes the end of the line.

Line 11

Both Plassart and Oliver agree on what can be restored.

Lines 12-16

These are too fragmentary to permit any restoration, and none has been attempted.

Line 17

Here we have]*eiase* followed by *entellomai*. Plassart treats *eia* as the end of one word, and *se* as the accusative of the personal pronoun. Oliver is not convinced, "If it were the dative *soi* to accompany *entellomai*, I would be more open to persuasion." (239). However, while the dative is the more normal, it is not obligatory; cf. BDF, n. 409(1). Oliver treats *eiase* as the end of a verb, but makes no suggestion as to what it might be; by itself it is the first Aorist of *eaô* 'to let go'. As he himself recognizes, his reconstruction means two juxtaposed verbs, which would be unusual, even if one were in a subordinate clause. None of these difficulties arise in the case of Plassart's hypothesis; the identical word order appears in Mk 13:34. On purely linguistic grounds, therefore, Plassart's restoration appears the more probable, and this controls the restoration of the second lacuna in line 7.

Line 18

This is the end of the inscription, and both Plassart and Oliver agree on the restoration.

BIBLIOGRAPHY

Texts

a) From the *Loeb Classical Library* (Cambridge: Harvard University Press). Grateful acknowledgement is made to the copyright holder for permission to reproduce the following translations:

Alciphron, Aelian, Philostratus: *Letters*, trans. by A. R. Benner and F. H. Forbes.

Antipater of Sidon, in *The Greek Anthology*, trans. by W. R. Paton.

Appian, *Roman History,* trans. by H. White.

Apuleius, *The Golden Ass,* trans. by A. Adlington.

Athenaeus, *The Deipnosophists*, trans. by C. B. Gulick.

Cicero, *Tusculan Disputations*, trans. by J. E. King.

——————————, *De Republica*, trans. by C. W. Keyes.

Crinagoras, in *The Greek Anthology*, trans. by W. R. Paton.

Dio Cassius, *Roman History*, trans. by E. Cary.

Dio Chrysostom, trans. by J. W. Cohoon and H. Lamar Crosby.

Frontinus, *The Stratagems and The Aqueducts of Rome*, trans. by C. E. Bennett and M. B. McElwain.

Josephus, *The Jewish War*, trans. by H. St. J. Thackeray.

——————————, *The Antiquities of the Jews,* trans. by H. St. J. Thackeray.

Livy, *History of Rome,* trans. by B. O. Foster, et alii.

Martial, *Epigrams,* trans. by W. C. A. Ker.

Pausanias, *Description of Greece*, trans. by W. H. S. Jones.

Philo, trans. by F. H. Colson.

Philostratus, *The Life of Apollonius of Tyana*, trans. by F. C. Conybeare.

Pliny the Elder, *Natural History*, trans. by H. Rackham, W. H. S. Jones, and D. E. Eicholz.

Pliny the Younger, *Letters and Panegyricus*, trans. by B. Radice.

Plutarch, *Moralia*, trans. by F. C. Babbitt, W. C. Helmbold,
    P. H. de Lacy, B. Einarson, P. A. Clement, H. B. Hoffleit,
    E. L. Minar, F. H. Sanbach, H. N. Fowler, L. Pearson,
    and H. Cherniss.
Polystratus, in the *Greek Anthology,* trans. by W. R. Paton.
Seneca, *Moral Essays,* trans. by J. W. Basore.
Strabo, *Geography*, trans. by H. L. Jones.
Suetonius, *Lives of the Caesars*, trans. by J. C. Rolfe.
Tacitus, *Histories and Annals*, trans. by C. H. Moore and J.
    Jackson.
Vitruvius, *De Architectura*, trans. by F. Granger.

b) From the *Collection "Budé"* (Paris: Société d'édition
'Les Belles Lettres'):

Cicéron, *Sur la loi agraire* (Discours, IX), trans. by A. Bou-
    langer.
Pétrone, *Le Satiricon*, trans. by A. Ernout.
Properce, *Elégies*, trans. by D. Paganelli.
P. Aelius Aristides, *The Complete Works*. Vol. II. *Orations
    XVII-LIII*, trans. by Charles A. Behr, Leiden: Brill, 1981.
    (Grateful acknowledgement is made to the publisher for
    permission to reproduce Or. 46:20-31).

Studies

Baird, W.
    1961   "Letters of Recommendation. A Study of 2 Cor
            3:1-3." *JBL* 80: 166-172.

Bagdikian, Anita
    1953   *The Civic Officials of Roman Corinth.* Unpub-
            lished   M.A.   dissertation,   University   of
            Vermont.

Banks, Robert
    1980   *Paul's Idea of Community.* Exeter: Paternoster
            Press.

Barrett, Charles Kingsley
   1958   *The New Testament Background. Selected Documents.* London: SPCK.

Bourguet, Emile
   1905   *De rebus Delphicis imperatoriae aetatis capita duo.* Montpellier.

Brassac, A.
   1913   "Une inscription de Delphes et la chronologie de saint Paul." *RB* 10: 36-53.

Broneer, Oscar
   1962a "The Isthmian Victory Games." *AJA 66: 259-263.*
   1962b "The Apostle Paul and the Isthmian Games." *BA* 25: 1-31.
   1971   "Paul and the Pagan Cults at Isthmia." *HTR* 64: 169-187.
   1973   *Isthmia*, vol. 2: *Topography and Architecture.* Princeton: American School of Classical Studies at Athens.

Broshi, Magen
   1975   "La population de l'ancienne Jérusalem." *RB* 82: 5-14.

Cadbury, H. J.
   1934   "The Macellum of Corinth." *JBL* 53: 134-141.

Caley, E. R.
   1941   "The Corroded Bronze of Corinth." *Proceedings of the American Philosophical Society* 8:689-761.

Carcopino, Jéróme
   1941   *Daily Life in Ancient Rome*, trans. by E. O. Lorrimer. reprinted London: Penguin Books, 1981.

Carney, Thomas F.
   1975   *The Shape of the Past. Models and Antiquity.* Lawrence: Coronado Press.

1979   *Content Analysis. A Technique for Systematic Inference from Communications.* Winnipeg: University of Manitoba Press.

Carpenter, Rhys
1929   "Researches in the Topography of Ancient Corinth - I." *AJA* 33: 345-360.

Comfort H.
1931   "The Date of Pausanias, Book II." *AJA* 35: 310-314.

Conzelmann, Hans
1967   "Korinth und die Mädchen der Aphrodite. Zur Religionsgeschichte der Stadt Korinth." *NAG* 8: 247-261.
1975   *1 Corinthians.* Philadelphia: Fortress Press.

Craddoxk, Paul T.
1982   "Gold in Antique Copper Alloys." *Gold Bulletin* 15:69-72.

Daniel, Jerry L.
1979   "Anti-Semitism in the Hellenistic Roman Period." *JBL* 98: 45-65.

Deissmann, A.
1926   *Paul. A Study in Social and Religious History.* London: Hodder and Stoughton.

De Waele, F. J.
1930   "The Roman Market North of the Temple at Corinth." *AJA* 34: 432-454.

Elliott, John H.
1981   *A Home for the Homeless. A Sociological Exegesis of 1 Peter, Its Situation and Strategy.* Philadelphia: Fortress Press.

Frazer, James G.
1913   *Pausanias's Description of Greece,* trans. with a commentary, vol. 3. London: Macmillan.

Furnish, Victor Paul
  1988   "Corinth in Paul's Time. What Can Archaeology Tell Us?" *BAR* 15/3:14-27.

Gebhard, Elizabeth R.
  1973   *The Theatre at Isthmia.* Chicago/London: University of Chicago Press.

Green, Peter
  1974   *Juvenal. The Sixteen Satires.* London: Penguin.

Haenchen, Ernst
  1971   *The Acts of the Apostles. A Commentary.* Philadelphia: Westminster Press.

Harris, W.
  1982   "'Sounding Brass' and Hellenistic Technology." *BAR* 8: 38-41.

Hennequin, L.
  1934   "Delphes (Inscription de)." *DBS* 2: 355-373.

Hill, A. E.
  1980   "The Temple of Asclepius: An Alternative Source for Paul's Body Theology?" *JBL* 99: 437-439.

Hock, Roland F.
  1978   "Paul's Tentmaking and the Problem of his Social Class." *JBL* 97: 555-564.
  1979   "The Workshop as a Social Setting for Paul's Missionary Preaching." *CBQ* 41: 438-450.
  1980   *The Social Context of Paul's Ministry. Tentmaking and Apostleship.* Philadelphia: Fortress Press.

Horsley, R. A.
  1981   "Gnosis in Corinth: 1 Corinthians 8.1-6." *NTS* 27: 32:51.

Jackson, F. J. Foakes and Lake, Kirsopp
  1933   *The Beginnings of Christianity.* Part 1. *The Acts of the Apostles.* Vol. 5. *Additional Notes to the Commentary.* London: Macmillan.

Jeremias, Joachim
  1966   *The Eucharistic Words of Jesus.* New York: Scribner's.

Jewett, Robert
  1979   *A Chronology of Paul's Life.* Philadelphia: Fortress Press.

Kent, John Harvey
  1966   *Corinth VIII/3. The Inscriptions 1926-1950.* Princeton: American School of Classical Studies at Athens.

Kraabel, A. T.
  1981   "The Disappearance of the 'God-fearers'." *Numen* 28: 113-126.
  1982   "The Roman Diaspora: Six Questionable Assumptions." *JJS* 33: 445-464.

Lang, Mabel
  1977   *Cure and Cult in Ancient Corinth. A Guide to the Asklepieion.* Princeton: American School of Classical Studies at Athens.

Larsen, J. A. O.
  1938   "Roman Greece," in *An Economic Survey of Ancient Rome*, ed. T. Frank. Baltimore: Johns Hopkins Press. 4: 259-498.

Levi, Peter
  1971   *Pausanias, Guide to Greece*, trans. with a commentary. London: Penguin Books.

Lisle, Robert
  1955   *The Cults of Corinth.* Unpublished Ph.D. dissertation, Johns Hopkins University.

Lüdemann, Gerd
  1980   *Paulus, der Heidenapostel.* Band 1. *Studien zur Chronologie.* Göttingen: Vandenhoeck und Ruprecht.

McEleney, N. J.
1973 "Conversion, Circumcision and the Law." *NTS* 20: 113-126.

Metzger, Bruce
1975 "The Nazareth Inscription Once Again," in *Jesus und Paulus* (Festschrift W. G. Kümmel). Göttingen: Vandenhoeck und Ruprecht. 221-238.

Meyers, Eric M. and Strange, James F.
1981 *Archaeology, the Rabbis, and Early Christianity.* London: SCM.

Millar, Fergus
1964 *A Study of Dio Cassius.* Oxford: Oxford University Press.
1966 "The Emperor, the Senate, and the Provinces." *JRS* 56: 155-166.
1981 "The World of the *Golden Ass.*" *JRS* 71:63-75.

Miller, Stella G.
1972 "A Mosaic Floor from a Roman Villa at Anaploga." *Hesperia* 41: 332-354.

Murphy-O'Connor, Jerome
1978 "Freedom or the Ghetto (1 Cor 8:1-13; 10:23-11:1)." *RB* 85: 543-574.
1980 "Sex and Logic in 1 Corinthians 11:2-16." *CBQ* 42:482-500.
1983 "Corinthian Bronze." *RB* 90:80-93.
1984 "The Corinth that Saint Paul Saw." *BA* 47:147-159.
1988 "1 Corinthians 11:2-16 Once Again." *CBQ* 50:265-274.

New Documents Illustrating Early Christianity
1981 Sydney: Ancient History Documentary Centre of Macquarrie University.

Oliver, J. H.
1971 "The Epistle of Claudius which mentions the Proconsul Junius Gallio." *Hesperia* 40: 239-240.

Oxford Classical Dictionary
Oxford: Clarendon Press.

Pemberton, Elizabeth G.
1981   "The Attribution of Corinthian Bronzes." *Hesperia* 50: 101-111.

Pfitzner, Victor C.
1967   *Paul and the Agon Motif. Traditional Athletic Imagery in the Pauline Literature.* Leiden: Brill.

Plassart, A.
1967   "L'inscription de Delphes mentionnant le proconsul Gallion." *REG* 80: 372-378.

1970   *Fouilles de Delphes III/4. Les inscriptions du temple du IV siécle.* Paris: Ecole Française d'Athénes. n. 286.

Plommer, Hugh
1983   "Scythopolis, Caesarea and Vitruvius: Sounding Vessels in Ancient Theatres." *Levant* 15:132-140.

Roux, Georges
1958   *Pausanias en Corinthie.* Paris: Belles Lettres.

Schürer, Emile
1979   *The History of the Jewish People in the Age of Jesus Christ,* vol. 2 revised and ed. by G. Vermes, F. Millar, and M. Black. Edinburgh: Clark.

Scranton, R., Shaw, J. W., and Ibrahim, L.
1978   *Kenchreai. Eastern Port of Corinth I. Topography and Architecture.* Leiden: Brill.

Shear, Theodore L.
1925   "Excavations at Corinth in 1925." *AJA* 29: 381-397.

1931   "A Hoard of Coins found in the Theatre District of Corinth in 1930." *AJA* 35: 139-151.

Smallwood, E. Mary
1970   *Philonis Alexandrini Legatio ad Gaium.* Leiden: Brill.

1981   *The Jews under Roman Rule from Pompey to Diocletian. A Study in Political Relations.* Leiden: Brill.

Smith, Dennis E.
1977   "Egyptian Cults at Corinth." *HTR* 70:201-231.
1980   *Social Obligation in the Context of Communal Meals: A Study of the Christian Meal in 1 Corinthians in Comparison with Graeco-Roman Meals.* Unpublished Th. D. Dissertation, Harvard University.

Theissen, Gerd
1982   *The Social Setting of Pauline Christianity. Essays on Corinth,* ed. and trans. with an introduction by J. Schütz. Philadelphia: Fortress Press.

Wilkinson, John
1974   "Ancient Jerusalem. Its Water Supply and Population." *PEQ* 106: 33-51.

Wiseman, James
1978   *The Land of the Ancient Corinthians.* Göteburg: Aström.
1979   "Corinth and Rome I: 228 B.C.-A.D. 267," in *Aufstieg und Niedergang der römischen Welt,* ed. H Temporini. Berlin: de Gruyter. VII/1: 438-548.

Wright, Kathleen S.
1980   "A Tiberian Pottery Deposit from Corinth." *Hesperia* 49:135-177.

Youtie, H. C.
1948   "The *Kline* of Seraphis." *HTR* 41: 9-29.

Ziegler, Konrat
1951   "Plutarchos von Chaironeia." *PW* 21: 636-962.

Abbreviations

AJA   *American Journal of Archaeology.*
BA   *Biblical Archaeologist.*
BAR   *Biblical Archaeology Review.*
CBQ   *Catholic Biblical Quarterly.*
DBS   *Dictionnaire de la Bible. Supplément.*
HTR   *Harvard Theological Review.*
JBL   *Journal of Biblical Literature.*
JJS   *Journal of Jewish Studies*
JRS   *Journal of Roman Studies.*
NAG   *Nachrichten von der Akademie der Wissenschaften in Göttingen.*
NTS   *New Testament Studies*
PW   Pauly-Wissowa, *Real-Encyclopädie der classischen Altertumswissenschaft.*
RB   *Revue Biblique.*
REG   *Revue des Etudes Greques.*

INDEX

CLASSICAL AUTHORS

SUBJECTS

NEW TESTAMENT